Chapaev

KINOfiles Film Companions

General Editor: Richard Taylor

Written for cineastes and students alike, KINOfiles are readable, authoritative, illustrated companion handbooks to the most important and interesting films to emerge from Russian cinema from its beginnings to the present. Each KINOfile investigates the production, context and reception of the film and the people who made it, and analyses the film itself and its place in Russian and world cinema. KINOfiles also include films of the other countries that once formed part of the Soviet Union, as well as works by émigré filmmakers working in the Russian tradition.

KINOfiles form a part of KINO: The Russian Cinema Series.

CHAPAEV

JULIAN GRAFFY

KINOfiles Film Companion 12

I.B. TAURIS
LONDON · NEW YORK

Published in 2010 by I.B.Tauris & Co Ltd
6 Salem Road, London W2 4BU
175 Fifth Avenue, New York NY 10010
www.ibtauris.com

Distributed in the United States and Canada Exclusively by Palgrave
Macmillan, 175 Fifth Avenue, New York NY 10010

ISBN: 978 1 85043 987 5

A full CIP record for this book is available from the British Library
A full CIP record is available from the Library of Congress

Library of Congress Catalog Number: available

Printed and bound in Great Britain by CPI Antony Rowe, Chippenham
From camera-ready copy edited and supplied by the author

Contents

Illustrations

Nos 1 and 2, the author's personal collection; Nos 3, 4 and 10, courtesy of the *Iskusstvo kino* archive; Cover and Nos 5-7, 9, 12, courtesy of Irina Filatova, Informbiuro, Lenfilm Studios; No. 8, British Film Institute; Nos 11, 13, courtesy of *Seans*, St Petersburg; No. 14, photograph of objects from the author's personal collection by Birgit Beumers; No. 15, Andrei Rogatchevski.

Acknowledgements

I am extremely grateful to Richard Taylor, and to Philippa Brewster at I.B.Tauris, both for inviting me to contribute this volume to the I.B.Tauris KINOfile series, and for their consistent encouragement and extraordinary patience while I was at work on it.

I wish to offer heartfelt thanks to the following people who helped me along the way, by supplying me with material and by answering my questions: Irina Petrova and Evgeni Tsymbal in Moscow; and Birgit Beumers, Rajendra Chitnis, David MacFadyen, James Mann, Milena Michalski, Rachel Morley, Andrei Rogatchevski, Amy Sargeant, Ol'ga Soboleva and Candyce Veal. All the mistakes that remain are my fault.

I owe, as ever, a huge debt of gratitude to the energy, good humour and resourcefulness of the staff of the Library of the School of Slavonic and East European Studies, University College London, and especially to Gillian Long.

Two great scholars of Russian film, Josephine Woll, in Washington and Rashit Yangirov, in Moscow, offered their advice and support as I was writing this book, but neither lived to see it published. I dedicate it to their memory.

Note on Transliteration

The transliteration system used for proper names in the text of this study is that of the Library of Congress, without diacritics, with the following emendations;

(a) when a Russian name has a clear English version, such as Eisenstein, Mayakovsky, that is preferred;

(b) when a Russian surname ends in -ii or -yi, this is replaced by a single -y, e.g. Shklovsky;

(c) when a Russian given name ends in -ii, this is replaced by a single i, e.g. Grigori.

The standard Library of Congress system is used in the Notes and the Further Reading.

Production Credits

Production company:	Lenfil´m, 1934
Release date:	7 November 1934
Directors:	Georgi and Sergei Vasilev
Screenplay:	Georgi and Sergei Vasilev, based on Dmitri Furmanov's novel *Chapaev* and other texts.
Co-director:	Iuri Muzykant
Assistant director:	Isaak Appel
Directors of photography:	Alexander Sigaev, Alexander Ksenofontov
Assistant cinematographer:	Apollinarii Dudko
Music:	Gavriil Popov and Beethoven's *Moonlight Sonata*
Sound:	Alexander Bekker
Production design:	Isaak Makhlis
Running time:	90 minutes

Cast:

Vasilii Ivanovich Chapaev	Boris Babochkin
Commissar Furmanov	Boris Blinov
Petka	Leonid Kmit
Anna	Varvara Miasnikova
White Colonel Borozdin	Illarion Pevtsov
Potapov (Petrovich), his Cossack orderly	Stepan Shkurat
White Lieutenant	Georgi Vasilev
White General	Vladimir Sladkopevtsev

Bearded peasant	Boris Chirkov
Elan, the Brigade Commander	Viacheslav Volkov
Zhikharev, the Platoon Commander	Nikolai Simonov
Vet	Mikhail Rostovtsev
Veterinary orderly	Emil Gal
Commissar Sedov	N. Medvedskii
Novikov, the Chief of Staff	N. Pozdniakov
Lanky partisan	Konstantin Nazarenko
Teresha	Georgi Zhzhenov

Chapaev is available on DVD with optional English subtitles from Krupnyi plan, Russia.

1. Chapaev the man, *Chapaev* the book

Who was Chapaev?

Vasili Ivanovich Chapaev is one of the most famous Red commanders of the Civil War, and one of the most fabled heroes of Russian history. He was born into a peasant family on 28 January 1887 in the village of Budaika near Cheboksary, a town on the River Volga to the east of Nizhny Novgorod, which was then in the Province of Kazan but is now the capital of the Chuvash Republic.[1] During the 1890s the family moved south, to the village of Balakovo near Nikolaevsk (now Pugachev) in Samara Province, between Samara and Saratov, on the eastern bank of the Volga. It was here that Chapaev had just under three years of schooling, and then worked as a carpenter. A frequently repeated tale of his youth is that while helping to build a church in a village near Nikolaevsk he climbed on to the cupola to set up the cross. After he had done so he fell to the ground, but was completely unharmed. For this he earned the nickname Ermak, after the legendary sixteenth-century Cossack leader who began the Russian expansion into Siberia, a comparison which would be developed by the Vasilev Brothers in their film.[2]

In November 1908 Chapaev was called up to the Tsarist Army, only to be demobilised six months later because of illness. In the autumn of 1914, with the outbreak of World War One, he was again called up, serving initially on the South-Western Front in Galicia. He took part in a number of important campaigns, and was promoted a number of times, becoming Sergeant Major in 1916. For his bravery he was awarded three George Crosses and a George Medal. Seriously wounded, he was sent back to Nikolaevsk at the end of 1916, and joined the 138th Reserve Infantry Regiment. During 1917 Chapaev became politically active, speaking at rallies and joining the Party Committee of his regiment. Eventually, on 28 September 1917, just before the October Revolution, he became a member of the Bolshevik

Party. Under his command the soldiers of the 138th Reserve disarmed their officers and on 14 December 1917 Chapaev was elected Regimental Commander. Two days later, at a District Congress of Peasant Deputies, he was elected Deputy Chairman of the Presidium, and in January 1918 he was named Military Commissar of Nikolaevsk. In early 1918 he led the First Nikolaevsk Battalion of the Red Army in putting down insurrections in local villages.

In late March 1918, Cossack forces loyal to the Whites led a rebellion in the town of Uralsk, on the Ural River to the east of Saratov and began to march on Saratov. Then in the summer the Czechoslovak Corps rebelled and together with White forces took Nikolaevsk. Throughout the year Chapaev led the local resistance to White offensives, retaking Nikolaevsk on 21 August. On 22 September he was made Commander of the newly formed Second Nikolaevsk Division

Chapaev surrounded by his men

and sent to harry the Whites at Uralsk. These skirmishes lasted for two weeks and the Reds suffered heavy losses, but Chapaev and his men eventually managed to break the siege. Since his reputation both as a courageous soldier and as a leader of men was growing all the time, the decision was taken to send Chapaev to study at the Staff Military Academy in Moscow. He joined the Academy on 3 December 1918, but was unhappy there. On 24 December he wrote to Gavriil Lindov, the Chairman of the Revolutionary Military Committee of the Eastern Front Fourth Army, and the man who had arranged for him to go to the Academy 'to increase his military knowledge', making a formal request to be transferred:

> I humbly request you to recall me to the headquarters of the Fourth Army for some sort of duty, as commander or commissar in any regiment, since the teaching in the academy is not of any use to me. What they are teaching I have experienced in practice. [...] And I am not prepared to languish within these walls to no purpose. It seems like a prison to me and I humbly beg you once more not to wear me out in this captivity. I want to work, not to lie around, and if you do not recall me I shall go to the doctor, who will let me off, and I shall lie around doing nothing. But I want to work and to help you. If you want me to help you, I shall be happy to be at your service.[3]

He was sent to Samara, where Mikhail Frunze, who had been made Commander of the Fourth Army, appointed him Commander of its Special Alexandrov-Gai Brigade. Then on 9 April 1919 he was made Commander of the 25th Rifle Division of the Fourth Army, the largest on the Eastern Front.[4]

   He fought successfully against the White troops of Kolchak's army under General Kappel. In the storming of the town of Ufa on 9 June, Chapaev was wounded but battled on, earning the Order of the Red Banner. In late June, when the White Cossacks again attacked Uralsk, Chapaev and his men were sent back to the Uralsk Front. They took the small riverside town of Lbishchensk with heavy losses, thus halting the White advance.

   But on the night of 4-5 September 1919 the Whites under Major General Borodin surrounded the town from three sides. In the ensuing fighting Chapaev was seriously wounded, but managed to escape to the Ural River. Here he was shot again, and here Chapaev died. There are several competing versions of these final hours: either he tried to swim across or he was carried on a raft by Hungarian Red soldiers. Either he died while crossing the river or he died just after reaching the other side. Some versions even suggested that Chapaev survived the White assault and lived to fight on, attesting to meetings with him months and years later. This was the beginning of Chapaev's legendary afterlife, a life which continues to this day.

Dmitri Furmanov
Dmitri Andreevich Furmanov, the writer of the novel *Chapaev*, was born in the village of Sereda in Kostroma province on 26 October 1891.[5]

   He entered Moscow University's Historico-Philological Faculty in

October 1912, specialising in literature and spending all his spare time reading. But with the outbreak of war he took a course as a medical orderly, qualifying (as a 'brother of mercy') in November 1914. At the end of the year he began to work on hospital train No. 209, and in January 1915 he met and fell in love with a young woman who was working on the same train as a 'sister of mercy', Anna Nikitichna Steshenko (whom he called Naia). In August 1918, they committed themselves to each other by drawing up what they described as a 'Project of loving-free-marital life', in which they agreed:

> We shall not burden ourselves with the conventions of bourgeois rules and the proprieties of marriage. We have had no betrothal, no wedding service, we have nothing but this constitution which we have freely established for ourselves.[6]

When, in 1919, Furmanov joined Chapaev's forces, Anna Steshenko went along too, to do cultural work among the soldiers.

After almost two years working on the train, Furmanov went back to Ivanovo-Voznesensk in October 1916 to teach workers. This brought him into close contact with Bolsheviks, and he greeted the February 1917 Revolution as a 'great festival for Russia'.[7] After the October Revolution he immediately began to work for the new revolutionary authorities in Ivanovo-Voznesensk. His conversations with Frunze, whom he met in December 1917, led to his joining the Bolshevik Party in July 1918.

When in January 1919 Frunze was put in command of the Fourth Army on the Eastern Front, Furmanov left for the Front with him. On 27 February 1919 he was ordered to go to Alexandrov-Gai, to join the troops being re-organised under Chapaev's command. When these troops were re-constituted as the 25th Rifle Division of the Fourth Army, Chapaev was appointed their Commander, and Furmanov was made their Commissar. The posts of political commissars in the Red Army had been set up by a decision of the Executive Committee of the Bolshevik Party of the spring of 1918. It was announced on 27 March that commissars would be given political control over the organisation and life of the army, and responsibility for the political reliability of military commanders and military specialists. The Commissars were given important powers, and no order could be put into practice without their signature.[8] A resolution of the Eighth Congress of the Bolshevik Party in March 1919 further indicated:

> Commissars in the army are not only the immediate and direct representatives of Soviet power but they are also above all the

bearers of the spirit of our party, its discipline, its firmness and courage in the struggle for the achievement of the goal we have set ourselves.[9]

Furmanov and Chapaev

Furmanov met Chapaev for the first time on 9 March 1919 but such was Chapaev's fame that he had already heard a great deal about him. Throughout the five months in which they worked together he used his diary to record his impressions of the Commander's words and actions, and of the reactions he provoked in others. Furmanov's diaries were his first attempt to articulate his understanding of the Chapaev phenomenon and served as raw material both for his novel and for the later film. He first mentions Chapaev in a long diary entry of 26 February 1919, in which he refers to him by his popular nickname, 'Chapai':

Here, throughout the region, you can hear about Chapai and his glorious Detachment. They call him simply Chapai. This word brings terror to the White Guard. Wherever they hear that he is approaching there is turmoil and panic in the enemy camp. The Cossacks disperse in terror, because there has apparently not been a single occasion when Chapai has been beaten. He is a completely legendary figure. Chapai's actions are marked by extreme independence; he hates plans and schemes of all kinds, strategy and other such military wisdom. He has only one strategy – a fiery, powerful blow.[10]

Thus even before the two men had met, Furmanov was influenced, for good and ill, by the Chapaev legend. When they did finally meet, on 9 March 1919, Furmanov noted down his further impressions:

This morning, at about seven, I first laid eyes on Chapaev. What I saw was a typical Sergeant Major, with a long moustache and greasy hair which was stuck down to his forehead; blue, understanding eyes and a decisive gaze. [...] Either he is quick-thinking, or he has a lot of good experience, but he works things out extremely quickly and understands things in a flash. [...] He speaks confidently, interrupts people, stops people, always speaking his own thoughts in full. He does not stand contradiction. His manner is simple, and with the Red Army soldiers even a bit coarse...
I noted that he likes to sing his own praises. He rates himself highly, knowing that his glory has resounded across the whole area, and he accepts this glory as his due.[11]

The selection of entries from Furmanov's diary presented in his 1960 *Collected Works* concentrates on his relationship with Chapaev, and contains many episodes and character assessments which will be familiar to readers of the novel and viewers of the film. On 13 March he describes Chapaev's approach to addressing his men in the following terms:

> For organised, conscious workers his ultra-demagogic approach would now be comic and even shocking but here, among his peasant Red Army men, it worked, and even had colossal positive consequences.[12]

He goes on to quote Chapaev telling his men that he would shoot anyone found stealing, and encouraging them to do the same to him, should he ever sink so low. He continues:

> I am your commander, but your commander only in battle; in our free time I am your comrade. Come to me at midnight or later, if you need to, wake me up, I shall always be ready to talk to you, say what is necessary. If I am eating, sit down and eat with me, if I am drinking tea, sit down and drink. This is the life I am used to. I have not been to any academies, or completed my studies there, but still I have formed fourteen regiments, and in each of them I was commander.[13]

A few days later, Furmanov admitted that Chapaev's personality had completely captured his attention and that he spent his time attempting to understand him fully.[14]

By 19 April he is calling himself Chapaev's shadow, in a diary entry entitled 'Chapaev and I' which makes it clear to readers that another of Furmanov's perhaps scarcely conscious purposes in keeping this diary is to promote his own effectiveness as political commissar, and to share Chapaev's glory:

> We have to decide all matters together. He does not discuss a single question without me, he takes advice about everything, he asks about everything. And thanks to that I am always informed about all enterprises and proposals. We have established the best, most trusting relations.[15]

On 19 May Furmanov writes that they have become so close that 'we cannot be parted for a day without pining'.[16]

His admiration also frequently spreads beyond Chapaev to the simple and courageous men under his command. Furmanov, in his own representation, is an integrated and admired member of the Division, able to have a positive effect on Chapaev: 'I have learnt to tame him completely, he who is untameable', he writes on 29 May.[17] Nevertheless, a long, self-lacerating entry of 8 June records a conversation with his wife, Anna Nikitichna (Naia), in which he informs her of his dissatisfaction with the role of Commissar, explicitly by comparison with that of Commander, and tells her of his decision (which he has already discussed with Chapaev) to ask to be transferred away from Chapaev's Division so that he can undergo further military training.[18]

When on 30 July a telegram arrives recalling him to Samara for other duties, Furmanov is no longer certain that he wants to leave, even persuading Chapaev to write asking for permission for him to stay, but the decision of the Revolutionary Committee of the Southern Group of Forces is not rescinded, and on 5 August, Furmanov and his wife leave.

Just over a month later news reaches Furmanov of the Whites' night attack on Lbishchenk. His initial diary reactions were written when the full scale of the tragedy was unclear, and he repeatedly expresses the hope that Chapaev has survived, but eventually he accepts that the 'free eagle' has died in the Ural River.[19]

Furmanov, Chapaev and Naia

The entries from Furmanov's diary presented in the 1960 *Collected Works* are extremely reticent about the role of his wife in the period of his campaigns with Chapaev. The first mention of her presence is in the 8 June 1919 conversation about his desire to become a Commissar, something that she does not think he would do well. Then, on 4 August, on the eve of their departure, he writes of her 'magnificent' work in the cultural-educational sphere, and says that her fellow workers were horrified to learn that she was leaving. But turning to later sources gives a fuller picture.

Anna Nikitichna had arrived at Chapaev's Division to engage in cultural and educational work on 18 April 1919, by which time her husband had already been serving there for six weeks, and was put in charge of a group of actors. According to her later memoir, Chapaev could not initially see the point of her activities, but he eventually became her warmest supporter and put out a special order compelling the commanders and commissars under his charge to assist her in every way.[20] But Pavel Kupriianovsky provides evidence that Naia was also the cause of a major rift between the two men during the month of June. Noticing that Chapaev was 'not indifferent to her', she had let him pay court to her and this had provoked Furmanov to jealousy. Kupriianovsky quotes an unpublished entry of 12 June from Furmanov's diary, entitled 'An Explanation with Chapaev.'

> Chapaev: 'You, comrade Furmanov, kept saying to me that my attitude to you has been tainted, this is not true, it is the same as it ever was, but your attitude to me really has been tainted. You are no longer speaking to me, you are angry with me, [...] Of course this is to do with Anna Nikitichna [...] I once told you that I would never make a play for the wife of a comrade. [...] It doesn't matter what I may have in my soul, no one can forbid me to love... I admit that I feel very warmly about her, that I find her very pleasant, but I have never spoken a word to her of love...

> Furmanov: And that was not why I changed my attitude to you, it was something else; my relations with you cracked after I became convinced that because of her you could weaken our cause, that because of her you had grown to hate me and grown completely cold to me.[21]

Relations between the two men worsened over the next few weeks, their conflict reaching its apogee at the end of the month. On 27 June Furmanov wrote an extraordinary letter to Chapaev, which, though it was apparently never sent, casts a searing light upon the true nature of their deteriorating relationship.[22] Furmanov announces that he is going to raise a 'large-scale case' against Chapaev and goes on to explain his reasons:

> You have been trying to put everything down to some absurd jealousy over Anna Nikitichna. Just think about it, it would be very funny and stupid if I really took it into my head to feel jealous of her because of you. Rivals like you are not dangerous. We have already had a good few such swains crossing our path, pressing their case, paying court, sending little love notes – but with all these swains she either spat in their face or sent them to the devil without any help from me. She showed me your latest letter where you write 'Your loving Chapaev'. She was really outraged by your lowness and brazenness and it seems that in her own note she did not express her contempt sufficiently clearly. I have all these documents in my possession and when the opportunity arises I shall show them to the

appropriate people so as to expose your foul game. There is no need to feel jealousy of base people, and of course I was not jealous about her, but I was profoundly outraged by your brazenly paying court to her and constantly pestering her, which was plain to see and about which Anna Nikitichna complained to me more than once. So it wasn't jealousy but outrage at your behaviour and contempt for your base and low tricks. Anna Nikitichna has been working with us for over two months, but did my contempt for you (what you call 'jealousy') also spring up two months ago? Not at all. I started feeling contempt for you just a few days ago, when I became convinced that you were a careerist, and when I saw that all your pestering her was becoming particularly brazen and offensive to the honour of my wife. I considered you to be a filthy and corrupt little man […] and the way you kept touching her left me with a feeling of revulsion. It was as if a white dove was being touched by a toad; I began to feel cold and disgusted. Well enough of that. When I need to I shall reveal the documents and provide a detailed exposure of all your baseness.[23]

He goes on to call him a coward, who had once been a brave fighter, but whose 'caution over your valuable life is very, very like cowardice'.[24] After threatening to have Chapaev 'thrown out of the Party and handed over to the Cheka', he ends his letter with the words: 'and don't forget that I have in my hands documents, facts and witnesses.'[25]

At the beginning of July the two men were summoned to Samara and reprimanded by Frunze.[26]

Though they apparently then grew closer again, the telegram which Furmanov received on 30 July, recalling him for other duties, was a direct response to the request for a transfer which he had expressed verbally during the conversation in Samara.[27]

In a diary entry written after he had learned of Chapaev's death Furmanov finally admits that the conflict between them was the main reason for his recall, and that that conflict was mainly caused by the fact that 'I could not completely destroy the jealousy that was boiling in my breast – I just didn't have the strength.'[28] The entry concludes with a bizarre declaration of love:

I repeat that the scandal happened with the close participation of Naia. If it had not been for her, this story would not have taken place; I have no doubt of that. And if this story had not taken place, then I would not have been recalled from the division. But if I had not been recalled from the division I would undoubtedly have perished with Chapaev, because I would not have left him for a minute […] It turns out that my life was saved by my beloved Naia, my good genius, my radiant fairy![29]

Though Furmanov included the story of Chapaev's falling in love with Naia and his own jealousy in some of the many plans he drew up for his novel, he eventually decided to discard the intimate aspect of Chapaev's adventures.[30] But the story of the love affair between Chapaev and Naia would continue to split audiences decades later.[31]

Furmanov's novel: composition and publication
In the years from 1919–22, Furmanov published a number of brief sketches of Chapaev's campaigns of 1919 and of the events in Lbishchensk which culminated in his death, but from the beginning of that year his thoughts turned to writing a 'big work' on the subject, using his diaries, newspapers, archives, and interviews with eye witnesses. His diaries for 1922 chart his fevered work on the novel. He cannot decide whether to give Chapaev his own name and whether to retain all his petty faults, or whether the novel should be driven by historical or literary concerns. On 29 October he lists possible genres for the project, ranging from memoirs to a historical ballad.[32] He offers various explanations of his approach, including the suggestions that Chapaev is a 'composite figure' and that the words spoken in the novel are both those which 'really' were spoken by the characters and others which 'were never spoken by them'.[33]

Furmanov wrote at great speed. By 4 January 1923 the novel was complete, and he began to worry about whether it would be accepted.[34] On 18 March 1923 Chapaev the novel appeared in print, published by the State Publishing House in Moscow. Another edition followed immediately and there was a third edition in 1925. In the last few weeks of his life Furmanov began radical revisions of the novel, managing to re-work the first seven chapters before his premature death. This fourth edition was published posthumously in 1926.[35] Though the novel would later provide the basis for the Vasilev Brothers' film, both the time of its composition and its manner of working were different and the contrasts between the novel and the film are as significant as the many continuities.

Furmanov's novel: structure and representation of Chapaev
Furmanov's novel begins in January 1919 in the town of Ivanovo-Voznesensk. Workers from local factories are off to join Frunze's troops fighting the White Admiral, Kolchak along the Volga. Among

them is a character based on Furmanov himself, a political worker here named Fedor Klychkov (in the novel Furmanov gives most of the real-life characters pseudonyms), though in the Vasilev Brothers' film he will be given Furmanov's own name. From the moment Klychkov arrives in Samara he begins to hear tales of Chapaev and his heroism, though significantly he also mentions Chapaev's faults.

As he travels through the steppe a local driver tells him tales of his encounters with Chapaev, leading Klychkov to his first passage of extended rumination about the man:

> Undoubtedy he's a popular hero, [...] a hero out of the camp of free men, Emelka Pugachev, Stenka Razin, Ermak Timofeevich. [...] He's precisely that, more of a *hero* than a fighter, more a passionate lover of adventure than a conscious revolutionary. [...] But what an original character he is against the background of peasant insurgency, what an original, bright, colourful figure![36]

This first assessment is interesting for a number of reasons. It associates Chapaev with two famous local Cossack rebels against Tsarist rule, Emelian (Emelka) Pugachev who rose against Catherine the Great in 1773, and Stepan (Stenka) Razin, who led a peasant uprising in 1670. Both 'Emelka' and 'Stenka' were defeated and put to death. Both became heroes of Russian popular culture. It further compares him to the sixteenth-century Cossack military leader Ermak, a comparison which will be extensively developed in the Vasilev Brothers' film. But at the same time it downplays Chapaev's role as a fighting man, an assessment from which the novel will not deviate.

Soon Klychkov receives instructions to go to the town of Uralsk, on the edge of the Kazakh steppes, where he meets Frunze, whose military prowess will, by contrast, be stressed in the novel, and Klychkov's propensity for hero-worship is first applied to him. Frunze sends Klychkov to do political work among Chapaev's troops and at this point Klychkov gives way to boyish excitement:

> With such a hero... shoulder to shoulder with Chapaev... how amazingly it had all turned out... [...] There I was dreaming about Chapaev as a legendary character, and suddenly to be together with him right by his side [...] Maybe we'll even get close to each other, become comrades?[37]

It is only in chapter five of the novel, after detailed reports on his encounters with other characters, that Klychkov finally meets Chapaev.

The physical description he gives here is of a very ordinary looking man, of average height, who does not appear strong and has slender, almost feminine hands. He observes Chapaev among his men, many of whom are named, including Petr Isaev, described as a slight young man who runs errands for Chapaev.

It is notable in this description of Klychkov's first encounter with Chapaev that he is troubled about seeming inexperienced, and he decides to turn all discussions with the Commander to questions of politics, where he is confident of his own greater knowledge. He sees again that Chapaev is a heroic figure:

> He embodies all the uncontrollable, elemental, angry force of protest that has built up among the peasants over a long time. But the elements – the devil knows where they can turn![38]

Klychkov decides, in a seminal application of the Soviet distinction between spontaneity and consciousness,[39] that he must take this elemental force under his ideological influence.

> He may be a popular hero, but what babyish ideas he has, this Chapaev! [...] He's a clever fellow, but he is terribly raw... he is going to take a long time to polish.[40]

The sixth chapter of the novel is devoted to the battle for the village of Slomikhinskaia. Its central concern is Klychkov's baptism of fire and the thoughts it provokes in him. He wonders if he will turn out to be brave or a coward, and he does actually turn tail, riding off out of danger from the heat of the battle. Skulking among the baggage trains he has plenty of time to reflect upon his cowardice and shame.

> Oh disgrace! Shame and disgrace! How ashamed he was to admit that in his first battle he had not shown enough spirit, that he had been cowardly as a kitten, had failed to justify his own hopes and expectations.[41]

This passage is remarkable, both because it shows Klychkov in formation, unlike the Furmanov of the film who is already an experienced fighter unthreatened by self-doubt, and because it suggests that despite the novel's title, it is Klychkov, his experiences and his observations, who is its central figure, and not Chapaev, a sense that will be borne out by later chapters.

After Klychkov has returned to the fighting men, the narrator informs us that very soon he would show exemplary bravery in battle, and be awarded the Order of the Red Banner. And then Klychkov hears Chapaev speak for the first time. Chapaev employs all his famous rhetoric and tells his full repertoire of tales. The soldier and peasant audience laps it up, but Klychkov is concerned at Chapaev's rash promises to his men, and decides that he too must make a speech, discussing the international situation and making subtle corrections to some of Chapaev's points.

The following chapters recount the battle against Admiral Kolchak's troops, and here the Divisional Commander, Chapaev, fades into the background, ceding the central place in the narrative to his Brigade Commanders, who take a more direct part in the fighting. Particular attention is paid to the talented and daring young Elan, who 'knows his own worth' and whose fiery recklessness leads him to resent the glory which has fallen to Chapaev's lot. 'Why should I not be Chapaev?', he asks, something which causes a froideur between them.[42] Elan does appear as a named character in the film, but in the film he knows his place.[43]

In the ensuing chapters of the novel more towns fall to the Reds. In Chapter 13 mention is suddenly made of Zoia Pavlovna, who is running a divisional troupe of actors, and is given a bouquet of flowers by Chapaev at the end of a performance at the municipal theatre in Ufa. Though this character is clearly based upon Furmanov's wife, Anna Nikitichna, no mention is made of this fact either here, or in the final chapter, Chapter 15, when she makes another appearance. The relief of Uralsk, in Chapter 14, is Chapaev's last major victory, and he is described as the hero of the day, but this is undercut by the narrator's mention in advance that Chapaev is about to die.

The last chapter is entitled 'Finale'. The division marches towards the town of Lbishchensk, joining up with Elan and his men who are desperately short of ammunition. Klychkov is suddenly recalled to Samara, to be replaced by Pavel Stepanych Baturin. Once again the narrator deflates any sense of dramatic uncertainty by telling us that this event will save Klychkov's life, since two weeks later Baturin would die 'for him and in his place'.[44]

Klychkov's imminent departure leads the narrator to an extended report of his concluding thoughts about Chapaev:

Where is Chapaev's *heroism*, where are his *heroic deeds*, do they really exist at all, and do heroes themselves exist? [...]
According to popular belief, 'Chapaev himself' was to be found unfailingly at the Front with his naked sword raised, Chapaev himself laid his enemies low, threw himself into the hottest

fighting and was responsible for its outcome. And yet nothing of the kind happened. Chapaev was a good and sensitive organiser for that time, in those circumstances, and for that milieu with which he had to deal, which had given him birth, which had raised him up. If times and people were even slightly different, we would not have known a popular hero called Vasili Ivanovich Chapaev! His glory was carried like down across the steppes and beyond by the hundreds and thousands of fighters who had also *heard of him* from others, believed what they had heard, been enraptured by it, embellished and added to it themselves through *their own* invention, and carried it further.[45]

Before his departure for Samara, Klychkov makes a final speech to the men, who, we are told, 'had come to love him and learnt to appreciate him in the last six months, valuing him especially for the fact that he knew how to curb Chapaev and *Chapaevism*.'[46] The Division continues its advance, eventually entering Lbishchensk. On the fateful night Chapaev informs his new young Chief of Staff Nochkov of rumours that there are Cossacks around and instructs him to put the divisional school of cadets on guard. Alas, in a turn of fate that remains shrouded in mystery, someone withdraws the guard, though Chapaev has given no such orders and Nochkov is above suspicion. The Cossacks sneak up by night and attack Chapaev's men. The reaction to the attack is represented as chaotic and panic-stricken, in direct contrast to Klychkov's repeated paeans to the importance of always being prepared and organised. Overwhelmed by superior enemy forces, Chapaev and his men retreat towards the river. Chapaev is hit in the arm but his orderly Petr Isaev is there to hep him down to the river bank. Just as he is about to reach the other bank, Chapaev is hit again, this time in the head, and he drowns in the Ural River. Petr fights heroically on, shooting six Cossacks before using his final bullet on himself. In the nearby village of Sakharnaia Elan finally takes charge of the Division, retreating through enemy lines by night and resisting when he can. Eventually Red reinforcements arrive from the north, force the Cossacks into retreat, and march on the town of Gurev on the Caspian Sea.[47]

Chapaev the novel and *Chapaev* the film
Chapaev was written at great speed by an inexperienced writer and this is no doubt the reason for its very obvious flaws. It is rambling and repetitious, inexcusably devoid of narrative drive, uncertain whether to be a first or third person narrative. It is heavily based upon

Furmanov's diaries, often quoting them verbatim, and like them (but unlike the film) it starts with the Commissar, not the Commander, with Klychkov discussing the legend of Chapaev, who is not introduced until Chapter 5. And despite the book's title, it is Klychkov who provides the novel's centre of gravity as Furmanov charts his gradual maturation from frightened neophyte into effective propagandist and confident fighting man.

The representation of Chapaev also differs greatly from book to film. In both works he is shown as flawed but, whereas in the film the flaws seem paradoxically to confirm his legendary status, the novel seems envious of his reputation and repeatedly determined to undermine it. Some of the differences can be explained by the gap in the times of the works' composition. In the early 1920s there was no model for narratives of the Civil War for Furmanov to consult, and so he relied in part on the example of nineteenth-century writers, in particular Lev Tolstoy. By 1934 the fame of Chapaev and other Civil War commanders had turned them into precisely the heroes of legend that Furmanov was attempting to analyse and, to some extent, debunk, and the Vasilev Brothers were able both to draw upon and to develop that legend. In the novel, Chapaev's spoken words were always filtered through the written words of Klychkov and his double the narrator, both of whom repeatedly inform the reader how lacking he was in coherence and verbal precision. The struggle of ordered, disciplined, conscious Klychkov to tame anarchic Chapaev was to a large extent a battle of language. In the words of Ronald Vroon about the novel, 'The general principle that equates oral discourse with what is false and written discourse with the truth is emplotted throughout *Chapaev*.'[48] In the film, by contrast, Chapaev's charisma is fundamentally dependent upon his being seen in action and given his own voice.

The two works also differ radically in terms of event and character. Most of Furmanov's long narrative of events of 1919 is jettisoned from the film, but several new episodes are invented. Names are changed – Klychkov is now called Furmanov and his replacement, Baturin, becomes Sedov. A key character in the novel, the Commander of the Fourth Army, Mikhail Frunze, is excised from the film, perhaps in part because of the rumour that his death on the operating table in October 1925 was organised by Stalin.[49] Many of the other commanders and ordinary soldiers who are named in the novel are absent from the film, and the role of Elan is dramatically diminished, consistent with the move to play up the legend of Chapaev the fighting man. There is also, understandably, no room in the film for the figure of Zoia Pavlovna, or any other character who might be connected with Furmanov's wife and rumours of a love affair between her and Chapaev. The role of Petr Isaev, on the other hand, is significantly developed into Petka, Chapaev's trusty sidekick, and he is allowed a touchingly chaste and doomed love affair with the invented character of Anna the fighting weaver. Other new characters are introduced, such as the White Colonel Borozdin and his batman, Potapov. The effect of these changes will be assessed later in this study.

Furmanov's novel: reception

The initial reception of the novel was encouraging, though one critic, Professor Girs, tempered his praise with the acute suggestion that 'the book might just as successfully have been called "Klychkov"'.[50] In 1925 Furmanov sent a copy of the book to Maxim Gorky, whose novel *Mother* had established a model for writing about the acquisition of revolutionary consciousness. Gorky's reply, while stressing that *Chapaev* is a 'very interesting and instructive book', offered detailed criticism of its shortcomings. Its artistic significance, he felt, was 'not at all high', and outweighed by its historical and pedagogical value. Formally it was neither a tale, nor a biography, nor even an essay, but 'something which violates all forms':

> I don't think I have to explain to you the enormous significance of form in art, its decisive significance. Every carpenter, when making a chair, is concerned that his chair should not turn out looking like a cupboard or a chest of drawers.[51]

But the most interesting of the reactions of writers to *Chapaev* is undoubtedly that of Isaak Babel, who had served as a war correspondent and a member of the Political Section of Marshal Budenny's First Red Cavalry on the Polish Front from June to September 1920. Like Furmanov, he kept a diary during his months at the Front and he drew upon it for the stories which began to appear in 1923 and would eventually be collected as *Red Cavalry*. Like Klychkov, the character whom Furmanov created out of himself in *Chapaev*, Babel's Liutov, another intellectual campaigning alongside Red Army men in the Civil War, has strong autobiographical elements. But, unlike Klychkov, who drowns his inferiority complex in a flood of revolutionary certainty, Liutov remains a neurotic and despised outsider. Furmanov chaired a discussion of Babel's *Red Cavalry* stories at Moscow's Press House on 29 November 1924.[52] The two men met for the first time on 17 December and then again on 19 December. The next day, Furmanov recorded in his diary Babel's lavish praise of the novel:

> It's a goldmine, he told me, *Chapaev* is my bedside book. I sincerely consider that there has so far been nothing like it about the Civil War. [...] I'll confess quite frankly that I borrow and snatch from your *Chapaev* in the most pitiless way.[53]

Babel and Furmanov continued to meet and correspond, and Furmanov was the editor of the first book edition of *Red Cavalry*, which appeared in May 1926.[54] By the time of the book's publication, Furmanov was dead, but the symbiotic relationship between *Chapaev* and *Red Cavalry* continued in the Vasilev Brothers' film.[55]

As the years went by, the novel's reputation grew. In 1926 S. Lunin published a dramatisation of it in six scenes, *On an Island of Bayonets (Na ostrove shtykov)*, which had its premiere (as *Chapaev*) at the First Theatre of Worker Youth in a working class area of Moscow the following year.[56] It was followed in 1928 by another dramatisation, A. Goriachy's *In the Whirlwind (V vikhre)*.[57] When in the early 1930s the debate began about the nature and history of Socialist Realism in Soviet literature, *Chapaev* was one of the works that was repeatedly invoked as a key precursor of the new orthodoxy. In the words of Katerina Clark, 'its ultimate role was to survive as a *model* work of Soviet fiction.'[58] With the coming of sound cinema, it was an obvious candidate to be turned into a film.

2. From book to film

Three months after the novel's publication, the Proletkino studio decided to film it and asked Furmanov to write a script.[1] He spent March and April 1924 on the project, reverting to earlier ideas by combining the tale of Chapaev's military exploits with the story of a love affair between the Commissar and an invented character called Ksanka.[2] In June he reported that though Goskino, the State Film Organisation had accepted the idea of the film they intended to 'do the script themselves', since his script had 'not used half the riches of

Sergei Dmitrievich Vasilev and Georgi Nikolaevich Vasilev

the book'. He thought that the film was going to be made towards the end of the year.[3]

But in 1924 the Soviet film industry was only just beginning to find its feet after years of disruption caused by Revolution and Civil War, so the project went into abeyance. In August 1925 Isaak Babel reported that in response to his enquiry at the State Film Factory [Studio] about why there had been no progress, he was told that all the State Film Organisation's energy was going into 'making the anniversary film "the year 1905"'. The new starting time for *Chapaev* the film was said to be spring 1926.[4] In the end *Chapaev* was not even the first of Furmanov's novels to be filmed. A version of his later novel *Rebellion* [Miatezh], about the struggle with rebels against Soviet power in Central Asia, directed by Semen Timoshenko, was released in 1929. There is some footage of the real Chapaev in a section entitled 'Under the Leadership of the Communist Party the toiling masses go to war', in Esfir Shub's 1927 documentary film *The Great Way* [Velikii put'],[5] but Furmanov's Chapaev would have to wait a little longer to reach the screen. In 1930-1, the writer's widow, Anna Nikitichna, wrote a second screenplay, which developed the epic dimension of the story (the script is largely written in blank verse) and the role of the masses, but downplayed the secondary characters, and, in the words of Iosif Dolinsky, turned the Commissar into a banal moraliser and Furmanov's novel into a 'dry poster'.[6] Then in the second half of 1932 Georgi Nikolaevich and Sergei Dmitrievich Vasilev were offered the chance of turning Furmanova's script into a film.[7]

The Vasilev "Brothers"

As their different patronymics indicate, the Vasilevs were not actually brothers, merely bearers of the same surname. They became "brothers" in an ironical reference in a 1928 article by Viktor Shklovsky,[8] adopting the pseudonym themselves for their 1932 film *A Personal Matter* [Lichnoe delo].[9]

Sergei Dmitrievich Vasilev was born on 4 November 1900 in Moscow, where his aged father was a military archivist.[10] His father died in 1907, and in 1910 Sergei moved with the rest of his family to St Petersburg, where in May 1915 he volunteered for the army, serving as a junior infantry officer from 1916. He returned briefly to Petrograd in early 1917 after being wounded, and then again in the autumn of that year. Just before the Revolution he joined the Red Guard, taking an active part in the events of October 1917 and in the later defence of the city. In May 1918 he was sent to Samara to fight against the Czech Interventionist forces, returning to Petrograd in January 1919, and then being posted to Odessa in the spring of 1920. In October he was recalled to Petrograd, where he served as adjutant to the administration of the City Commandant, but he was determined to return to his studies and in October 1921, though continuing to serve in the military, he entered the Petrograd State Institute of Screen Arts. During the early 1920s he had various small acting roles, but he eventually decided to try to become a director. He graduated from the Institute in February 1924, and in order to advance his ambitions, he moved to Moscow in May, taking up work as a film editor at the Sevzapkino studio.

Georgi Nikolaevich Vasilev was born in Vologda on 25 November 1899, the son of a court investigator. Having finished his schooling in Astrakhan in 1917, he studied briefly at Warsaw Polytechnic University, which had been evacuated to Nizhny Novgorod on the Volga. In 1918 he returned to Astrakhan and got a job in the Municipal Supply Committee, but in January 1920 he joined the Red Army, taking part in the fighting against General Kolchak. He was sent by the army to study in Moscow in 1922, and was demobilised in 1923. Like his namesake he also studied acting, joining the 'Young Masters' studio, run by the actor Illarion Pevtsov, in 1922. A young actor whom Vasilev met at the studio, Boris Babochkin, would later be cast in the title role in *Chapaev*, while the head of the studio, Pevtsov, would play the part of the White Colonel, Borozdin.[11] At the same time Georgi wrote film reviews for a number of newspapers and magazines and worked as a croupier at a NEP casino to finance his studies. Realising that he did not want to be an actor, he, too, took work as a film editor, in the Moscow offices of the State Film Organisation, in 1924.

Sergei Dmitrevich Vasilev recalls their meeting in the following words:

> Something amazing happened! An article appeared in the magazine *Soviet Screen* signed by 'Editor Vasilev'. I had not written it. What was going on? It turned out that I had a namesake working in the same profession, only at the State Film Offices. Of course I just had to meet him. [...] Soon, when all the film organisations were brought together as single unit in 'Sovkino' we began working under the same roof. From that day we were inseparable. We would sit opposite each other at the editing table and we learned to understand each other implicitly. We often worked in tandem on the same film.[12]

As well as preparing the 'Brothers' for a career in film direction, the years they spent cutting and re-editing foreign films earned them a reputation as expert editors. Sergei Dmitrievich recalls that Sergei Eisenstein and Grigori Alexandrov spent hours with him at his editor's desk when they were beginning work on editing *The Strike*. In the autumn of 1928 the Brothers joined Eisenstein's 'Instruction and Investigation Studio'. Sergei Dmitrievich also lectured on editing at the State Film School in Moscow and in Leningrad, and published a popular editing manual, *Montazh kinokartiny* [Film Editing] in 1929.[13]

The Brothers got their first chance to work more creatively when in 1928 they were asked to edit into a film the footage shot by cameramen on the three Soviet ice-breakers, including the legendary *Krasin*, sent to rescue the survivors of Umberto Nobile's airship, the *Italia*, which had crashed on the ice near the North Pole on 25 May. The film was released in the Soviet Union on 23 October 1928 under the title *Glory in the Ice* [Podvig vo l´dakh], and abroad under the title *White Mystery*.

In February 1929 they moved to Leningrad to begin work on their first feature film, *The Sleeping Beauty* [Spiashchaia krasavitsa, 1930] at the Leningrad Soiuzkino studio, which would later become Lenfilm studio. Based on a semi-autobiographical script by the future director Grigori Alexandrov, it provides a political history of Russia from before the Revolution to the present day through the life of a provincial theatre. Varvara Miasnikova, whom Sergei Vasilev married that same year, and who would later be cast as Anna in Chapaev, plays the part of a young revolutionary. The film gets its title from the fact that at its conclusion, despite fundamental social and political change, the theatre is still staging Tchaikovsky, though the film-makers consider his ballets to be of no interest to post-Revolutionary audiences. It was released on 21 October 1930, but was neither a critical nor a popular success and only three reels survive.[14]

After the failure of *The Sleeping Beauty*, the Brothers spent a long time looking fruitlessly for a more congenial script. Eventually, in 1931, they agreed to film a story about a worker who comes to accept the new Soviet order which, after many script changes, acquired the title *A Personal Matter*. The hero is a highly religious old metal worker who eventually agrees to melt down his church's bells for use in the construction of an ice-breaker.[15] It follows the 'coming to consciousness' structure of a number of books and films of the period, among the most famous of which is Vsevolod Pudovkin's *Mother* (1926), based on the novel by Maxim Gorky. *A Personal Matter* was released on 24 April 1932 but was not well received, and it was eclipsed by the appearance later that year of *Counter-Plan* [Vstrechnyi, directed by Fridrikh Ermler and Sergei Iutkevich], another film about a skilled old factory worker and his gradual acceptance of Soviet power.

Chapaev: from script to film

At the start of the 1930s it was repeatedly stressed that the Civil War, which had already provided the subject of a number of Soviet stories and films of the 1920s, was an appropriate subject for Soviet art. On 30 July 1931, at the suggestion of Maxim Gorky, the Party Central Committee promulgated a resolution 'On the publication of the story of the Civil War for the broad working masses.'[16] Nikolai Beresnev's film adaptation of Alexander Fadeev's novel *The Rout* [Razgrom], released two months later, on 10 September, told the story of heroic resistance to an attack by Japanese Interventionist forces.[17] The First All Union Conference for workers in the area of military and defence films was held on 15-19 May 1932 and concluded that the widespread opinion among artists that the Civil War theme was no longer relevant was dangerous and absurd.[18] And the eighth issue for 1932 of the newly founded journal *Proletarskoe kino* [Proletarian Cinema] carried an editorial with the following words:

> Have we got any films about how the *partisan* and *semi-partisan* detachments *were welded by the Bolshevik Party into the regular Red Army*? Where has the heroic work of the Party in creating the glorious victories of the Red Army been reflected?[19]

This was the context in which the Vasilev Brothers began work on the script of *Chapaev*. They had at their disposal Furmanov's diaries and notebooks given to them by his widow, and other archival materials. They made a trip to Lbishchensk, the scene of the tragedy. The initial stage, the 'literary script', took them about six months. As the script progressed they moved further and further away from both the novel and Furmanova's version. In the words of Dmitry Pisarevsky:

> Of the 57 scenes in the final version of the script only four (the clash with the vets, Chapaev's speech at the meeting, the attack on Lbishchensk and the death of the hero) were taken directly from the book, and went into the film, if in a changed form.
> 53 scenes were written *anew*.[20]

They introduced a number of characters not present in earlier versions, notably Anna the weaver and the White Colonel, Borozdin, and developed the role of others, in particular that of Petka.[21] The events of Furmanov's novel used in the film take place in a variety of settings and over a period of a full year from the attack on the White Czechs in September 1918 to the death of Chapaev in September 1919, but in the film both time and place are necessarily simplified to give thematic coherence and the sense of a seamless succession of events.[22] Above all, the powerful tensions between the two men, which are seen to boil over on occasion both in the novel and in Furmanov's diaries, are now significantly played down. Summing up their method in an article written a few weeks after the film's appearance, the Brothers insisted that:

> We consider that really bringing a literary work to the screen means knowing how to understand the feelings, thoughts, direction of the writer, and, while taking this as a starting point, to make use of additional material to create something new. This new thing must have an independent artistic life. [23]

In an article written in 1938 about the 'defence theme' in Soviet cinema, Sergei Vasilev reiterated the brothers' conviction that the Civil War theme had needed a new approach:

> The point turned out to be not that the viewer had no wish to see the Civil War on screen, but that he was sick of the clichéd devices and primitive methods with which it was being shown. […] So when we started work on *Chapaev*, we set ourselves the task of trying to show the Civil War by other means, other devices, of approaching it in a different way from what had been done before.[24]

In the early 1930s, Soviet studios were making sound and silent film simultaneously. Though *Chapaev* seems unimaginable to modern viewers as a silent film, and the Brothers saw it from the start as a sound film, it was entered into the studio's production plan as silent, and initially they could get no one to read and approve their script. Eventually they persuaded Mikhail Pavlovich Shneider, the studio director, to read the sound version. Though he too became convinced that it should be made as a sound film, he explained that Boris Shumiatsky, the head of the Soviet film industry in the 1930s, had categorically forbidden them to make a sound film. So they took the script to Moscow and got it read at the State Cinema Directorate [GUK], but when they returned to Leningrad they were once again told that it must be made as a silent film, probably because all the Lenfilm facilities for making sound films were already in use. The Brothers refused to be cowed and eventually, with the intervention of high-up military men, the decision was rescinded. These arguments delayed the start of filming for several months.[25]

Work on location began near the town of Kalinin in the summer of 1933 but appalling weather meant that they could complete only two days filming. Requests to move to a new area were refused. On their return to Leningrad they were told they had wasted so much money that work on the film would be stopped. Eventually they filmed the studio scenes over the winter, and went back to Kalinin in summer 1934 to shoot the exteriors.[26] But they also used the winter of 1933-4 to make further changes to the script, and they re-cast the roles of Petka and the unnamed but important character of the lanky partisan who rebels against Chapaev.

The final cast of the film included actors from a wide range of backgrounds. In addition to Babochkin and Pevtsov, Nikolai Simonov, who played the Platoon Commander, Zhikharev, and Mikhail Rostovtsev, in the part of the vet, were established theatrical actors. For Boris Blinov, an actor at the Leningrad Theatre of the Young Actor, Furmanov would be his first cinematic role. Emil Gal, who played the veterinary orderly, was a member of the FEKS [*Factory of the Eccentric Actor*] group, and had acted in the films of Kozintsev and Trauberg. Stepan Shkurat, on the other hand, who played White Colonel Borozdin's Cossack batman Potapov, had worked as a stove-setter and taken part in amateur theatricals before being noticed by Alexander Dovzhenko and offered the part of Opanas, the hero's father, in *Earth* [Zemlia, 1930]. The casting of some of the minor roles is particularly imaginative. The theatre student and former circus artiste Georgi Zhzhenov, in the role of the young weaver, Teresha, became a big popular star and made his last film appearance in 1998. Most remarkably, the bearded, middle-aged peasant who asks Chapaev whether he is for 'the Bolsheviks or the Communists' was played by the 33-year-old Leningrad theatre actor Boris Chirkov, who that same year created the role of the young Bolshevik, Maxim, alongside Chapaev the other legendary hero from the Revolutionary period in Soviet cinema of the 1930s, in Kozintsev and Trauberg's *The Youth of Maxim* [Iunost' Maksima, 1934].[27] Also fundamental to the film's success was the contribution of the composer, Gavriil Popov. Popov had studied both piano and composition at the Leningrad Conservatoire in the early 1920s. His lyrical music for *Chapaev*, and his arrangement of the song 'Black Raven' attracted enormous praise.[28]

Georgi Vasilev reports that work on editing *Chapaev* began on 20 September 1934. It was completed on 22 October and the film was handed over to the Lenfilm Studio Directorate, who approved its release.[29] On 27 October it was send to the State Cinema Directorate for the next stage in its journey towards Soviet screens. According to

Sergei Vasilev, Shumiatsky watched it twice and demanded two changes. The Brothers considered that agreeing to one of these, the removal of the scene of the 'psychic attack' by White officers, would ruin the film, and they threatened to have their names taken off the credits.[30] They told Shumiatsky that if he put his instructions in written form they would make the changes they agreed to and bring the film for a re-showing. They knew that the authorities wanted the film to be released for the seventeenth anniversary of the Russian Revolution, on 7 November. The Brothers returned to Moscow on 2 November. Cunningly they delayed their arrival in Shumiatsky's office until just before the next showing, to a Commission of the Central Committee, was about to begin. To Shumiatsky's question 'Well, did you cut out what I ordered?' Vasilev replied that they had done as they had agreed. The Party Commission watched the film and approved it in its current form, so the outmanoeuvred Shumiatsky had to concede that it could pass on to its final hurdle, the Kremlin showing that was customary in those years. On 4 November, the Politburo member Kliment Voroshilov instructed the Brothers to remain in the State Cinema Directorate and await his call. According to Sergei Vasilev, Voroshilov had told Stalin that the Brothers were anxiously awaiting a decision, but Stalin had replied 'maybe we shouldn't call them over yet, maybe the film is bad and we are going to criticise it. They are nervous people.' But at 1:00 in the morning, after he had watched the first two reels of the film and knew that he liked it, he gave Shumiatsky instructions to summon the directors.[31]

The first public showing of the film was at the Titan Cinema in Leningrad on 5 November 1934. The official release date was the anniversary of the October Revolution, 7 November.

3. *Chapaev* the film

Plot synopsis

In the early summer of 1919 the Russian Civil War is raging. In the area to the East of the River Volga, the partisans of Chapaev, the Commander of the 25th Rifle Division of the Fourth Red Army, are joined by the Commissar, Furmanov, and his Red Army volunteers, who are weavers from the nearby town of Ivanovo-Voznesensk. Petka, Chapaev's orderly, immediately falls for Anna, one of the weavers, while giving her a lesson is assembling a Maxim gun. At the White HQ Colonel Borozdin, who is in charge of the Urals Cossack forces, discusses Chapaev's reputation as a leader of men with a young lieutenant of the army of General Kappel.

Two of Chapaev's men complain to Furmanov that Chapaev wants to have a peasant vet from his village made a doctor. Furmanov explains to a furious Chapaev why this is not possible and tells him why he should set an example to his men.

Colonel Borozdin's orderly, Potapov, explains to him that his brother, Mitia, has been condemned to death for attempting to go over to the other side, but Borozdin is prepared only to reduce the punishment to one hundred lashes.

The peasants complain to Furmanov that some of Chapaev's partisans are robbing them. Furmanov has Zhikharev, their platoon commander, arrested. Chapaev is again furious, but Furmanov stands his ground, reminding the Commander that it is the Party that has sent him to join the Division. When the peasants thank Chapaev for the return of their stolen goods, he begins to trust Furmanov's advice and tells his men that he will shoot them if there is a recurrence of looting.

Petka goes out into the night to prove himself to Anna by capturing a White prisoner, who will then be interrogated about the Whites' battle plans. He finds Potapov, but, learning that the man's brother is dying, lets him go. An angry Chapaev initially threatens to send him to a military tribunal.

That night, while Colonel Borozdin plays Beethoven, Potapov informs him that his brother has died. Later he goes over to the Reds and tells them that he has overheard that the Whites are planning a 'psychic attack', though neither he nor Chapaev knows what this means. Chapaev and Furmanov plan their strategy. At the beginning of the psychic attack, in which General Kappel's officer regiment advances on the Red partisans on foot, intending to terrify them with their mad daring, some of Chapaev's men lose heart and try to go home, but Chapaev shoots the ringleader on the spot. When the Whites come within range, Anna responds with machine-gun fire, and later when the White Cossacks attack they are routed by Chapaev. The Reds take over the Kappel Brigade's headquarters.

In the autumn Furmanov is recalled to other duties and replaced by Sedov, which greatly upsets Chapaev. Colonel Borozdin plans a new attack on Chapaev's isolated HQ in the small town of Lbishchensk. On the night of 5 September 1919, as Chapaev and his men lie sleeping, Borozdin makes his surprise attack. Chapaev sends Anna off for reinforcements as he and Petka attempt to hold back the advancing Cossacks. Chapaev is wounded and Petka carries him down to the Ural River to make his escape. While Chapaev is swimming across the river, Petka falls dead on the shore. Chapaev too eventually sinks beneath the waters. Chapaev's Brigade Commander, Elan, leads a counter-attack. Colonel Borozdin is killed and the Whites are routed.

The film's opening sequences: introduction to the main characters
To the evocative music of Gavriil Popov, the film's credits announce that *Chapaev* has been made from a script by the Vasilev Brothers based on materials by Dmitri and Anna Furmanov. The film opens dynamically with a troika rushing from the back of the frame through a broad steppe landscape, to the ever more insistent sound of the bells of its three horses.[1] The combination of this sound and the depth and breadth of the landscape immediately suggest to Russian viewers, in the words of Sergei Vasilev, 'something close and familiar',[2] an impression further heightened by the lighting, which evokes 'the light tones of a summer, sunny day'.[3] A motley band of men rush towards the carriage from the front of the frame. When the two groups meet we see that the coach is carrying Chapaev, immediately distinguished by his moustache and the Caucasian fur hat [*papakha*] which he will wear throughout the film, his peasant orderly, Petka, and, behind them in the carriage, a Maxim gun.[4] Chapaev stands up on the cart and, raising

his hand, he stops these men, his partisan division, one of several which sprang up at the time, in their tracks. A tall, lanky young man, who will not be named in the film, but who will have a number of further dramatic encounters with his Commander, explains that the Czechs have forced them from the farmstead they were occupying.[5]

The Czechoslovak Corps was first set up in 1914, and consisted of Czechs working in Russia who decided to join the fight against Germany. Later it was expanded through the recruitment of Czech and Slovak prisoners of war from the Austro-Hungarian Army. In March 1918 the Bolshevik Government gave the Corps, now 40,000 strong, permission to leave the country by going east along the Trans-Siberian railway, so as to continue the fight against Germany. As they were making their way across the country, fighting broke out between Czech troops and Hungarian prisoners of war in Cheliabinsk, which led the Soviets to attempt to disarm the Corps. This in turn led the Czechs to rise against Soviet power, and fighting between the Czechoslovak Corps and Red forces began on 25 May 1918, starting in Western Siberia, but soon spreading west along the railway line. In June 1918, the Czech troops passing through Samara were persuaded to join the Socialist Revolutionary underground in fighting the local Bolsheviks and soon they liberated large areas of the Volga region from the Bolsheviks. The last Czechs would not leave the country until November 1920.[6]

Chapaev's reaction is immediate. Using the familiar form of address ('*ty*' rather than the formal '*vy*'), something which Trotsky described as permissible for a commanding officer only 'to express close comradely relations', he sends the man off in search of the rifle he has abandoned.[7] This first encounter between Chapaev and his men shows the dynamic energy with which he is able to rouse them to counter-attack and the mix of affection and respect tinged with fear in which they hold him. They rush to a bridge occupied by the Czech soldiers, taking them unawares. With their uniforms and their guns, the Czechs initially seem a more disciplined force than Chapaev's partisan band, but they are hugely outnumbered by the advancing men and intimidated by the noise of the Maxim gun which Petka fires, under Chapaev's instruction, directly from the back of the carriage. This image, of Petka, Chapaev and the legendary Maxim gun, is one of several of what Daniil Dondurei calls 'posed' shots in the film, and it immediately figured on one of the film's contemporary posters.[8] In the words of Jeremy Hicks, in contrast with Furmanov's desire to examine and question the Chapaev cult, the film begins with a dramatic picture of Chapaev the figure of myth:

It introduces us to the character by giving us an example of Chapaev's legendary power, showing him photographed from a low angle directing Pet´ka's machine- gun fire, inspiring fleeing soldiers to return to the battle even without their rifles. The low angle shot is clearly chosen to heighten the spectator's sense of Chapaev's charisma [...]⁹

Chapaev and Petka prepare to rout the Czechs

The Czech forces are swiftly routed, some fleeing across the bridge, and others running through the shallow river. After a brief fade to black, a device that will be repeatedly used to link the film's episodes, Chapaev's men are seen lined up in an open field of the re-captured farmstead as their commander talks to them, revolver in hand. The dual nature of his relationship with them, which combines approachability with a readiness to be tough when necessary, is stressed once again, as he first thanks them for driving out the Czechs, their first martial victory, but then returns to the question of their abandoned weapons. The lanky young man, it emerges, has thrown his rifle in the river in panic. When he rushes off to retrieve it, we see that he is barefoot. Another man, Pastukhov, says that he has hidden away his machine gun 'purposely', implying that he intended to keep it safe. A third shuffles awkwardly to conceal the fact that he has no rifle. Brandishing a whip, Chapaev announces that that evening he will inspect them.

Petka and Chapaev are on the captured bridge, Petka sitting with his legs dangling over the river and Chapaev leaning on the railing deep in thought. We hear the distant sounds of singing men. *Chapaev* was one of the first Soviet sound films, and contains a number of songs, all of which contribute to the film's dramatic power. This first of them, *Ei, po doroge*, is a traditional Cossack song, with words altered for use as a marching song by the Red Army.

> Ei, po doroge, ei, po doroge!
> Po doroge voisko krasnoe idet!...
> Gei, eto sila, ei, eto sila,
> Eto sila, sila groznaia idet!

> Hey, along the road, hey, along the road!
> The Red troops march along the road!...
> Hey, it's a force, hey, it's a force,
> Hey it's a threatening force marching!

Like Chapaev and Petka, these men emerge from the back of the frame, but their uniforms and their ordered, disciplined marching contrast strikingly both with the hectic dynamism of Chapaev's first appearance and with the headlong zigzags of his own ragged band. The man at their head comes on to the bridge and tells Chapaev both his name and his role. He is Furmanov and he has been appointed as Commissar of Chapaev's division. The troops he has brought with him are army volunteers, weavers from the nearby industrial town of Ivanovo-Voznesensk. This is the first encounter of the two forces at the centre of the film's plot, Chapaev and Furmanov, the Commander and the Commissar, country and town, peasant energy and Party discipline.[10] Chapaev is embarrassed that the Commissar has arrived at the very moment when his men are rushing about looking for their weapons. He wastes no time in showing Furmanov his distrust, eventually offering a grudging handshake and muttering 'I know' before turning back to lean on the bridge.

Simple-hearted Petka approaches one of the weavers and slaps 'him' on the back, only to be amazed that this Ivanovo-Voznesensk weaver is a woman, Anna, a character who did not figure in Furmanov's novel but was added by the Vasilev Brothers for the film.[11] When Petka discovers his mistake he smiles broadly. Anna smiles in return and asks whether he is the machine-gunner. Petka's reply, 'I can also be a gunner', the first words we hear him speak, conveys the sense of his own capacity that will be associated with him throughout the film. Back at the bridge, Chapaev grudgingly admits the timeliness of the reinforcements, since he has received orders to go on to the offensive the following day. Chapaev is still slouching as he says these words, and Oksana Bulgakova, in a fascinating study of gesture and movement in the film, identifies this scene as establishing both his 'too free and easy' bearing and his contrast with Furmanov:

> He is not standing in a military manner, he is sprawled out, leaning on the bridge railing with one foot stuck out. This careless pose of the Commander is contrasted with the military bearing of the civilian Furmanov, who becomes embarrassed at his own 'formality' and immediately copies Chapaev's pose so as to make some contact with him.[12]

Furmanov asks what the men are doing, scrambling around in the river. Chapaev's reply, 'They're swimming... it's hot', echoes the peasant cunning of his men's excuses to him, and is the first of several occasions in the film when he will use his native wit to get out of a spot.

Lessons in tactics
The troops are sitting around relaxing in a broad village street. Some of them are eating at a field kitchen, others singing a jolly ditty 'Come to me, my handsome' ['Prikhodi ko mne, milenok']. Chapaev's partisans are making friends with the weavers, distinguishable by the red stars on their *budenovki*, the pointed cloth helmets named after the Red Cavalry Commander Semen Budennyi that identified them as members of the Red Army. Petka emerges from a hut and fires his revolver to get their attention. 'Quiet, citizens', he says, 'Chapaev is going to think' ['Tikho, grazhdane! Chapai dumat' budet']. These are perhaps the most famous words in the film, implying that thinking requires the Commander's special concentration, and are now used ironically about people considered none too bright, but they are only one of dozens of sentences from the film that have entered popular currency.[13] Impressed by the power of his words, Petka sits down on the steps of the hut.

Inside the hut the commanders are poring over maps. Novikov, the Chief of Staff, outlines a plan for taking the village of Lomikhinskaia the following morning, his reference to the dispositions of the 'Pugachev' and 'Razin' regiments inscribing the current struggle into the heroic history of rebellion in this area against Tsarism.[14] Furmanov is not among the men seated at the table. He stands behind them, craning to get a view. Chapaev asks his Brigade Commander, Elan, for his tactical ideas, and then, cunningly, asks what 'the Commissar' thinks. Furmanov is now seen for the first time with a pipe in his mouth, a pipe which will be associated with him in other key scenes in the film, both suggesting that he is an intellectual and associating him implicitly with the Soviet Union's most famous pipe-smoker, Joseph Stalin.[15] After first hesitantly playing for time, Furmanov deftly dodges Chapaev's question, in part because he does not want to appear to challenge Chapaev's authority so soon after his arrival, but mainly because he is astute enough to see that Chapaev is setting him a trap. The question is not genuine, since Chapaev has, as Furmanov notes, already made a 'different' and 'correct' decision as to how the village will be captured. Making ostentatious measurements with a compass handed him by Petka, as if to give a scientific underpinning to his decision, Chapaev finally announces with a dramatic flourish (using another phrase which has entered the language, and which was improvised by the actor, Boris Babochkin) 'Well what you have just been saying should be spat upon and forgotten!' ['Nu, na to, chto vy seichas govorili, naplevat´ i zabyt´'], before announcing how the battle will in fact be fought.

The skirmish, though unseen, was clearly successful, since the conversation is followed by an intertitle transferring the action to 'The captured village'. There is a poster of a Red Army soldier, rifle in hand, on the back wall of the room in which Chapaev is lounging on a sofa, noisily munching an apple. In the foreground, by contrast, Furmanov sits at a table peeling potatoes. Elan bursts into the room, his left arm grandly bandaged in a sling. Chapaev bluntly calls him a fool for letting himself be wounded, insisting that 'my fighting deputy' should have had the wit to keep out of the way of a 'foolish bullet'. Elan's modest protest that it was hardly his fault leads to a lesson in tactics from his commander. In one of the most famous scenes in Russian film history, Chapaev rushes impulsively to the table. Using the potatoes which Furmanov has been peeling to represent 'our detachment' and its commander, the apples to represent the enemy, Furmanov's pipe (unceremoniously removed from his mouth) as cannon fire and Elan's cigarettes as machine guns, he repeatedly asks where the commander should be ['Gde dolzhen byt´ komandir?'] at different stages of the battle. He suggests that the Commander should always be concerned to protect himself, so as to command his troops another day, and at one stage the vegetable bowl does duty as 'some vantage point in the rear' to which he should retreat so as to lead his men to final victory, a victory dramatically signified by sweeping the apples on to the floor. Yet in this particular tactical discussion, observed with wry amusement by Furmanov, the last laugh is on Chapaev. 'You're lying, Vasili Ivanovich', says Elan, 'if it's necessary you're always in the front!'[16]

In another of the scenes set in the open air which subtly remind viewers just what is being fought over, Petka and Anna are sitting under the resplendent branches of a tree.[17] Petka, echoing his commander, is giving a lesson in warfare, this time attempting to explain to Anna the intricacies of the workings of the Maxim gun. The first self-powered machine gun, it was invented by Sir Hiram Maxim in 1884 and used successfully by the British in several late nineteenth-century colonial wars, inducing both Rudyard Kipling, and Hilaire Belloc to write sardonic lines about its martial effectiveness.[18] Versions of the gun were made in a number of European countries, including Russia. It was used by Russian troops in the Russo-Japanese War, the First World War, the Civil War and even the Great Patriotic War of 1941–5.[19]

'Where should the Commander be?'

Petka names the parts of the gun, beginning with the 'back plate' ['zatylnik'], only to be interrupted by the lanky partisan, sitting watching on the homestead fence. Winking at him to go away, and not to cramp his style, Petka names the second part, the 'cheeks' ['shchechki']. As he does so, he grabs Anna's breast and attempts to kiss her.[20] Anna pushes him away and mockingly calls him a 'hero'. She refers with irritation to the self-importance she has encountered among Chapaev's men, and suggests that their 'heroism' is confined to their exploits with women. Stung by this, Petka insists that he will, indeed, show himself to be a hero, by creeping into the Whites' camp and capturing a 'iazyk' (a 'tongue', a prisoner who will talk).

Petka teaches Anna to use the Maxim gun (production still)

This explicit allusion to the nature of heroism takes place in the context of broad contemporary discussion of the subject in Soviet society. The title of 'Hero of Labour' had been instituted in 1927 and that of 'Hero of the Soviet Union' on 16 April 1934, while *Chapaev* was in production. It was first awarded, at a Kremlin reception hosted by Stalin, on 2 May, to the fliers who had saved the crew of the *Cheliuskin* from their ship frozen in the Arctic ice. Petka's promise here is that he, an ordinary peasant, can also be a hero.[21]

Stung by Anna's sarcasm, Petka starts packing up the gun, but Anna insists that he continue the lesson. There is a sticky moment as Petka has to explain that the part he is showing her really is called the cheeks...

In the White camp

In a passenger train on a siding in a provincial station, two officers are sitting in a staff carriage. One, who will remain unnamed, is a young lieutenant, dressed in the black uniform of the troops of General Kappel. The other, a balding older man, is Colonel Nikolai Sergeevich Borozdin, who is in charge of the Urals Cossacks forces.[22] These two characters, neither of whom was present in Furmanov's novel, represent the two groups of soldiers who constitute the White enemy in the film. The staff carriage is considerably better appointed than the peasant hut in which Chapaev and Furmanov have just been seen, and throughout the film the Whites will be predominantly associated with relatively luxurious interiors and the Reds with exteriors, with Russian nature. The young lieutenant, played by one of the film's directors, Georgi Vasilev, examines a map and recalls fighting on the German Front against the legendary General von Ludendorff, an experience which makes him consider Chapaev, a former sergeant major, to be an unworthy opponent. His irony is, however, challenged by the wiser older man, who realises that both Chapaev and his considerable reputation as a fighter represent a real danger to White ambitions. Differences between the two men also arise over Borozdin's treatment of his Cossack orderly, Potapov, whom he refers to familiarly by his patronymic, Petrovich. Borozdin questions the lieutenant's implication that his treatment of his orderly is too patriarchal. He insists (ironically using a Latin phrase which, along with his unmilitary bearing, inevitably links him to the old world) that it is utterly contemporary, since 'tempora mutantur'. The figure of Colonel Borozdin was widely seen to display a new maturity in the characterisation of the White enemy, who had hitherto been represented in caricatural form in Soviet art as devious, callous and cowardly. In part this was the result of the nuanced playing of the experienced theatrical actor Illarion Pevtsov in the role. Pevtsov wrote in his notebook in 1933, at the time when work on *Chapaev* was beginning:

> By the very nature of things, an actor cannot be a prosecutor or a defence counsel for the character he is playing. [...] He should always bear in mind that in nature   there are no pure black or pure white colours.[23]

One of the most widely used stratagems of *Chapaev* is that of doubling, of characters and of relationships. The relationship between Chapaev and Furmanov was echoed in a subsequent scene by that of Petka and Anna. Now the fatherly attitude which Chapaev assumes towards his orderly, Petka, is echoed and contrasted in the relationship of Colonel Borozdin and his orderly, Potapov. They have served together on several Fronts since 1914, and Potapov, who brings his master a cup of hot tea during this scene, knows exactly how much sugar to put into his glass. Borozdin is confident that he has no reason to look over his shoulder. But relations between master and man will alter radically in the course of the film.

Chapaev and Furmanov clash
Two agitated men, an elderly veterinary doctor and a young veterinary orderly, burst into the room where the strategy lesson had taken place. They complain to Furmanov, to his evident amusement, that Chapaev has demanded that they test a horse doctor from his native village and draw up a 'document' giving him permission to work on humans. When they refused to do so, he called them 'sons of bitches' and threatened to shoot them. Before Furmanov can respond, the door is again thrown open and a furious Chapaev rushes in, calls them 'enema pipes' and makes them march out in terror. Realising that he will get no support from the Commissar, he accuses him of supporting the 'rotten intelligentsia' and demands to know why not a single peasant is allowed to become a doctor. In his comic rhetoric he develops a position recently advocated by Lenin. In a brochure completed on 1 October 1917, 'Will the Bolsheviks hold on to State Power?', Lenin had written:

> We are not utopians. We know that any manual worker and any cook are not capable now of taking on the running of the state [...] But [...] we demand an immediate break with the prejudice which says that only rich officials or officials from rich families are capable of *running* the state, of carrying out the mundane, daily work of running it. We demand that *training* in the matter of running the state be carried out by conscious workers and soldiers and that work be begun on this immediately, that is to say that a *start* be made immediately on attracting all the workers, all the poor to this training.[24]

Chapaev's contempt for what he sees as the 'rotten intelligentsia' was also shared by Lenin, who wrote in a letter to Maxim Gorky of 15 September 1919:

> [...] worker and peasant intellectuals are growing and growing stronger in the struggle to overthrow the bourgeoisie and its

accomplices, the little intellectuals [*intelligentikov*], the lackeys of Capital, who imagine themselves to be the brains of the nation. In fact they are not the brains but the shit.[25]

Furmanov remains calm in the face of this onslaught, even allowing himself a mocking allusion to Chapaev's mispronunciation of the formal word 'document'. Sensing that he is being mocked, Chapaev lifts up a stool and throws it to the ground in fury, prompting Furmanov to reply, in an allusion to Nikolai Gogol's play *The Government Inspector*, that will of course be lost on Chapaev but caught by some members of the film's audience, 'Alexander the Great was also a great commander. But why break stools?'[26] Alexander the Great is known in Russian as Aleksandr Makedonskii, a name which Chapaev has never heard before, though he knows of Garibaldi, Napoleon and Suvorov (the very mention of whose names subtly places him in exalted company). He demands to be informed about this other great commander, since what Furmanov knows, he should know too. He explains that he has only known how to read for two years, another phrase calculated to endear him to those large sections of the audience who have themselves only recently become literate. But before Furmanov can begin to speak of Alexander, Chapaev begins to sing. It is striking that the songs sung by Chapaev and his troops are not the songs of revolution. Instead he sings:

Ty, moriak, krasivyi sam soboiu,
Tebe ot rodu dvadtsat´ let...

You are handsome, sailor,
You are twenty years old...[27]

This is the fourth encounter between Furmanov and Chapaev, and so far he has not risked giving him instruction. But, sensing that the Commander's fury has passed, he embarks upon the mentoring role for which the Party has sent him here.[28] Yet it is not politics that concerns the Commissar most at this point. Rather (and we recall that the scene had opened with Furmanov polishing his shoes) he is bothered that Chapaev is always so scruffy.[29] He tells him, 'handsome sailor', to smarten up a bit, now that he is a commander of the regular Red Army, and to give an example to his men. Though Chapaev cannot resist asking whether Alexander the Great wore white gloves, and how Furmanov might know anyway, he laughs, and the men whom Grigori Gachev has described as fire and the cooling water of reason, as 'organism' and 'mechanism', seem to be reconciled.[30]

Borozdin and Potapov

In Borozdin's second scene he is again sitting in the luxuriously appointed staff carriage, quoting with approval to a well-fed man in a civilian suit Lenin's contention that 'A strong home front determines final victory.' His willingness to praise his enemy as a military tactician is another way in which this White officer is rendered more positive for Soviet audiences, and his admiration for Lenin is a characteristic he shares with Chapaev. That Borozdin praises Lenin and not Trotsky, who in 1919 was People's Commissar for Army and Navy Affairs but who is never mentioned in the film, is of course motivated by the political context of the 1930s, evidence of the Stalinist rewriting of history.

While the Colonel is talking, his orderly, Potapov, pushes past the sentry and bursts into the room, his incursion completely at odds with his smooth, respectful entry in their previous scene. Silently, he proffers his master a note:

Report to the Group Commander:
At dawn today the Cossack of the first squadron of the Plastunsky regiment Dmitri Potapov was arrested while attempting to go over to the enemy.

The note also bears the instruction 'To be shot', over the signature of Colonel Borozdin. Looking it over, Borozdin mutters to 'Petrovich' about discipline and directives from HQ, taking refuge behind the nostrum that 'an order is an order'. But Potapov is not satisfied and gestures to him to look again. Only now does Borozdin recognise the surname which in his 'contemporary' treatment of his orderly he does not use, and asks whether the man is a relative. When Potapov replies that he is his brother, Borozdin's companion looks up from his newspaper, *Amur Life* [*Priamurskaia zhizn*] to see what approach he will now take (for an order is an order). Shamefacedly Borozdin mutters 'why didn't you say so earlier?' He crosses out his former instruction and begins to write another, the Cossack batman watching him over his bald head. The screen fades to black.

Who is head of the division?

An intertitle announces that Chapaev's division is advancing. Furmanov and some of the weavers have been billeted in the village school, its walls decorated with pictures. It is night time and Furmanov is lying on a bed in his shirt sleeves reading when a young weaver, Teresha, bursts in and tells him that there is disorder in the village, that lads from the third platoon are plundering the peasants' property. The furious Commissar immediately orders the arrest of the platoon commander, Zhikharev.

In the village the lanky young man who had lost his rifle at the start of the film has stolen a pig from an old peasant woman. When she complains that 'we waited and waited for you, but you are dragging off our last possessions. So this is what Soviet power is!', he replies: 'Quiet, gran, in wartime even a piglet is a gift from God.' The woman's words are echoed by a bearded, middle-aged peasant who has observed the scene:

> What a mess it all is. It's just like a merry-go-round. The Whites come and rob us, the Reds come and rob us. What is a peasant supposed to do? [...] 'Our boys are coming, hurrah, hurrah!' Now you have your 'hurrah'! We got what we were waiting for, damn it...

The very choice of the word merry-go-round contains a pithy indictment of the concept of revolution.[31] The peasants' complaints that the Reds robbed them, and that they were indistinguishable from the Whites, were first articulated in Furmanov's novel. Isaak Babel, a great admirer of the novel, put similar sentiments into the mouth of the eponymous Jewish stallholder hero of his story about the Red Cavalry 'Gedali'.[32] For Gedali there was no difference between the Poles, who abused him, and the Reds, who beat the Poles and then requisitioned his gramophone under threat of shooting. Liutov, Babel's hero, tries to explain to Gedali the moral difference between shots fired by Revolution and Counter-Revolution, but Furmanov, in the Vasilev Brothers' film, prefers actions to words. Now dressed in full uniform, he cross-examines Zhikharev. Initially the platoon commander is disdainful. Waving his whip, he smirks and says he knows nothing about any looting. When Furmanov orders his volunteer weavers to arrest him, Zhikharev, who shares Chapaev's hypertrophic sense of his own importance, exclaims: 'Arrest who? Me... a military commander?!' and reaches for his revolver. But Furmanov turns out to be quite capable of disarming him. He makes him write an order telling his men to return everything that they have plundered and a puny, bespectacled weaver locks him up.[33]

When Chapaev and Petia, who have learnt of developments, charge into the school building, Furmanov signals to Teresha to take off the note. The power struggle between Furmanov and Zhikharev is now repeated between Furmanov and Chapaev, who of course interprets the arrest of 'my fighting comrade' as an attack upon his own authority. His distrust of intellectuals is evident once more as he asks Furmanov how he dared to do this and calls him a 'soul of paper'. But when he attempts to liberate Zhikharev, he finds his way blocked by the bespectacled weaver. Furmanov too, it turns out, has his loyal lieutenants. The two groups that must combine to form a division of the Red Army, the weavers and the partisans, are still at odds.

Never one to eschew a dramatic gesture, Chapaev removes his overcoat and his fur hat, his belt, his sabre and his revolver and casts them to the floor. He undoes the neck of his tunic. He asks rhetorically: 'Who is head of the division, you or I? ['Kto khoziain divizii, ty ili ia?'], to which Furmanov replies, sardonically, 'You... and I' ['Ty... i ia']. This makes Chapaev even more furious and he retorts:

> I am Chapaev! Do you understand that I am Chapaev! But you... Who are you? Who sent you here? Do you want to paint yourself in someone else's glory? Get the hell out of the division![34]

Furmanov, always still in the face of Chapaev's dynamism, calmly answers that he does not need Chapaev's glory and that he can be dismissed only by those who sent him, by the Party, making the clash of forces represented in this scene utterly explicit. Standing under a portrait of the aged Lev Tolstoy, he tells Chapaev that as a Communist he should understand this.

Before Chapaev has a chance to reply, the bearded peasant comes into the school room. He asks which of the men is Chapaev and, initially unsure that a man who looks so scruffy can be the Divisional Commander, he thanks him for the return of all the peasants' property. Thus ironically it is Chapaev, not Furmanov, who is 'painted in someone else's glory'. Repeating his fears about a merry-go-round of Reds and Whites, the peasant thanks Chapaev 'in the name of society' and leaves the hut.

Once again, after a volcanic outburst, Chapaev calms down. Once again he has learned a lesson from Furmanov. He refuses Zhikharev's request to be released. Doing up his tunic button, he asks the Commissar to call a meeting. Disarmingly, however, he still finds a way of interpreting events that flatters his own ego. When Petka sings the praises of the Commissar, who has turned out to be a much more substantial fellow than he had first thought, Chapaev retorts that they would hardly send a nonentity to Chapaev!

It is the contradictions in Chapaev's character that make him so believable and so attractive to audiences. In the previous scene he had displayed the unformed, undisciplined side of his nature, emotional, vain and quick to take offence. At the meeting he stands imposingly stern and tall, shot from below, dressed smartly for effect:

> He goes out to the people in full fighting uniform, covered in straps.What doesn't he have on him; a sabre, on whose hilt he sometimes rests his hand, a leather whistle case on his chest, spurs on his polished boots, a map-case, a holster [...] Of course this ammunition has no practical or utilitarian significance at this moment. [...] The meaning of such imposing military dress is now different, purely aesthetic: it must make an *impression* on the fighters – not just inspiring them with the glory of victory but also disciplining them with threats.[35]

Chapaev speaks eloquently of the shame that the looters have brought on the division and the entire Red Army. Warming to his theme and daring to use words with which he is not entirely at ease, 'exploitation', 'capital', he insists that the fame of the *Chapaevtsy*, of which he is so proud, must not be associated with banditry. He is ready (like Borozdin) to order the shooting of anyone found breaking his rules but (unlike Borozdin) he will do the shooting himself. But if he is their 'commander' in battle, he is their 'comrade' at all other times, a man, like them, of little schooling, always ready to share his food or a glass of tea. This is an artful speech, playing explicitly on his dual nature, tempering severity with accessibility, and it wins over both his men and the assembled peasants.[36] Yet the bearded peasant, who had previously seen no difference between the Whites and the Reds, is still perplexed as to whether Vasili Ivanych is 'for the Bolsheviks or the Communists'.[37] It is important that Chapaev answer this question correctly, for the allegiance of the middle peasants [*seredniaki*], those who owned a little property, was of particular interest to the new regime. In Lenin's words, of November 1918:

> The middle peasant is not our enemy. He has vacillated, is vacillating and will vacillate [...] We must know how to reach an agreement with the middle peasant, without for a moment renouncing our struggle with the rich peasant (*kulak*) [...] this is the task of the moment, because it is precisely now that it is inevitable that   the middle peasant turn in our direction [...][38]

Only momentarily discountenanced, Chapaev pronounces himself 'for the International.'[39] But he still has to field one more question. Furmanov, who has sat smiling approvingly and drawing on his pipe through this entire scene, now wonders whether his pupil is for the Second International or the Third.[40] Here, too, however, Chapaev's peasant resourcefulness does not desert him. He asks which one Lenin is in. Learning that he is in the Third, which he founded, Chapaev announces that he, too, is for the Third.[41]

Petka the hero
To the ever more insistent ticking of a clock, Anna is in a peasant hut, assembling the machine gun. She completes her task before the alarm clock rings, to the delight of her 'teacher', Petka. Placing his arm around her, but without the coarseness which had marked their earlier 'lesson', he tells her that her studies are over and 'You and Maxim are now friends.' This nocturnal scene in which a woman works and her man looks on in admiration, has a powerful sense of naturalness and domesticity, but it also contains a strong, if latent erotic charge. Petka moves off to the window, hung with embroidered curtains, and looks out into the night. As he opens the window we hear the beautiful lyric theme which Gavriil Popov composed for the film, which will continue to play till the end of the sequence. Petka returns to the discussion of heroism begun in their previous scene together. He tells Anna that he is about to do what he had then boasted of, to go out and capture a White, who will be able to tell them about the enemy's plans. Once again, Anna wonders if he is capable of doing this, but this time her question is motivated by concern. Once again, but somehow without his earlier boastfulness, Petka assures her that 'I can do everything.' He stops at the door and turns back. The erotic tension in the scene increases as he returns to Anna. The audience, and perhaps Anna herself, imagine that he is going to kiss her, but Petka, like his master, is learning the virtues of restraint and self-control. Silently he shakes her hand before striding out into the night.[42]

The lengthy, wordless scene which follows is one of the most remarkable in the film. To the continuing sound of Popov's music, Anna rushes out after her man. As she watches him disappear into the distance, the camera shows us the landscape through which he is passing, broad cloudy skies, trees, a large expanse of water, a scene of Russian nature at its most beautiful.[43] Here, even more than in the film's opening scene, audiences can see what Chapaev and his men are fighting for. This moment of rest at the film's mid-way point prepares us for the dramas to come.

In the next sequence, set at dawn, Petka captures Potapov, who is fishing in a river. When the Cossack batman reaches for his gun, Petka tells him 'I took the bullets out, uncle' and tells him not to try any tricks. But Potapov explains, to the sounds of the dawn chorus, that he wants to make his favourite fish soup for his brother, Mitka, who is dying after having been lashed with ramrods. The solemnity of his endeavour is marked by the fact that he is wearing the George Cross and medal that he has won in battle, and Petka is moved to pity.

Petka prepares to capture a White (production still)

In a dramatic device used more than once in the film, the resolution of this encounter becomes clear only in the following scene. Chapaev and Furmanov are sitting together in the school room. Behind them are a blackboard, with a caricature of a priest, and a large map of the world. In front of them is Petka. It is a measure of Furmanov's growing confidence in Chapaev that he says not a word while Chapaev threatens Petka with a military tribunal for letting his prisoner go. It is a measure of Petka's own maturation that he willingly accepts this sentence. True heroism, it transpires, lies not in acts of daring, but in the readiness to make your own judgement in support of those who are suffering, and to take the consequences. Chapaev also knows this, of course, and he follows his threats with an affectionate reprimand to Petia for looking so scruffy. Using exactly the words he has learnt from Furmanov, he reminds him that as 'a conscious fighter in the regular Red Army', he 'should set an example to others'.[44]

Potapov changes sides
In the staff carriage, Colonel Borozdin is playing a grand piano. As the sounds of the first movement of the *Moonlight Sonata* swell out, his faithful batman sways in motion with the music as he polishes the floor with a foot cloth. Borozdin knows this piece by heart and plays without a score.[45] His love of this Beethoven sonata is another way in which he is connected to Lenin, who considered Beethoven's *Appassionata* to be the greatest music ever written, but who was famously mistrustful of the sentiments it aroused in him. As Maxim Gorky wrote in his obituary of the Bolshevik leader:

> One evening, in Moscow, in E.P. Peshkova's flat, Lenin heard the Beethoven sonatas played by Isai Dobrovein and said:

> > I know of nothing better than the *Appassionata*, I am ready to listen to it every day. It is amazing, inhuman music. I always think, with what is probably naïve pride: these are the miracles that can be achieved by man!

> And screwing up his eyes and with a bitter smile he added, gloomily:

> > But I can't listen to music often, it works on my nerves, I want to say sweetly stupid things and run my hand over the heads of the people who can create such beauty while they live in filthy hell. But now you can't run your hand over anyone's head, they'll bite your hand

off, you must beat people about the head, beat them mercilessly, although ideally we are against all violence against people.⁴⁶

Suddenly Potapov sees the document which Borozdin had signed, commuting his brother's sentence, and his expression darkens. As the music gains in momentum, the Colonel's vulnerability is emphasised by a number of close-up shots of his neck and of the short stubble on the back of his bald head. Suddenly we hear what sounds like a shot. Borozdin turns round to find that his batman has dropped his broom. So far the entire scene has been wordless, but now Potapov says: 'He's

Colonel Borozdin plays the *Moonlight Sonata*

dead... my brother! Mitka is dead!' Just as the commitment to high culture signified by the piano in the officers' quarters in *The Battleship Potemkin* did not prevent them from participating in the shooting of the rebellious sailors, so Borozdin can combine love of Beethoven with a readiness to ordering the beating of a soldier with ramrods of which Lenin would have been proud. The colonel slams the piano shut, the dull thud exposing his earlier boasts about his relationship with his batman as empty cant. Though he was initially represented with nuance, the Vasilev Brothers here show themselves ready to blacken his character significantly. This process will accelerate in the course of the film, and by its end he will be represented as a venal coward, raising questions about the consistency of the portrayal of his character and about the genuineness of his initially 'positive' portrayal.

Outside the Red camp, two sentries are on night duty. The older partisan explains to the younger Red Army man about Chapaev's peasant origins, his martial exploits, and his closeness to Frunze. Suddenly the younger man hears a rustling in the bushes and fires his gun. Furmanov emerges from the darkness. He praises them for not sleeping, but adds that if they are going to shoot, they should make sure to hit their target.[47] Then another man appears. It is Potapov, still wearing his George Cross. He explains that, after 'your lad' had let him go, he had decided to come over to the Reds himself. Cross-examined by Chapaev he reports that the next day there will be an attack by General Kappel's officers' units, an attack which he has heard described, in a word he does not know, as 'psychic' [*psikhicheskaia*]. Petka's act of mercy is now entirely vindicated. Smiling he takes Potapov, whom he calls 'brother-uncle' [*brat-diadia*] off to the kitchen. His choice of words is significant. If Borozdin had been exposed as a 'false father' to Potapov, the constant use of the words brother, uncle, granddad by Chapaev and his men underlines the fact that they are represented in the film above all through the metaphor of family.[48]

Chapaev sits poring over a map, planning his strategy. He asks the Commissar what he thinks. The words that he uses, 'kak dumaet komissar?', are exactly those he had used at the start of the film, but this time he genuinely wants to know. Furmanov offers his view in some detail, and repays the compliment by asking 'kak dumaet komandir?', what does the Commander think? Chapaev's reply is terser: 'OK, we'll meet them.' Furmanov goes off to discuss matters with his Communists. Chapaev is left alone. 'Psychic', he says, savouring the unfamiliar word, 'To hell with it! Make it psychic!'

Hours later, the Commissar has the map spread out on the floor. Now in his shirtsleeves, he is stretched out over it, as if through direct physical contact he could somehow understand more about the coming attack. He sings the first verse of an old Russian song:

Chernyi voron, chernyi voron,
Chto ty v´esh´sia nado mnoi?
Ty dobychi ne dobesh´sia,
Chernyi voron, ia ne tvoi!

Black raven, black raven,
Why are you weaving above me?
You will not get your booty,
Black raven I am not yours!

This is one of the two most important songs in the film, both of them dense with symbolic implication for the development of the plot, and it is remarkable that both of them, rather than speaking of the heroic exploits of the revolution, make melancholy, doom-laden reference to earlier pages of Russian history. It was originally written by the soldier poet Nikolai Verevkin on 14 May 1831 after the battle of Ostrelenka during the Polish uprising, and published in the journal *Russkii invalid* on 8 September 1831. At this point it was called 'Pod zelenoiu rakitoi' ('Under the green broom bush'), and redolent of official Russian patriotism. During the second half of the nineteenth century these elements were removed in versions of the poem sung among Cossacks and soldiers. It was reworked again during the Civil War and the Great Patriotic War.[49]

A yawning Petka tries to persuade Chapaev to go to bed, only to be asked whether he is the 'Government Inspector' or the 'Sleep Commissar'. The easy banter between the two men is reminiscent of a late night conversation between father and son, and the confiding atmosphere is adumbrated by the softness of the lighting. Petka tells the Commander admiringly that he is 'a person inaccessible to my reason' and calls him 'Napoleon. A real Napoleon!', the second time the name of the great general has been spoken in connection with Chapaev. Unembarrassed by this comparison, Vasilii Ivanych retorts that Napoleon had it easy, with no machine guns and planes to contend with. He adds that he was sent a plane a few days ago, but that it uses so much petrol that you cannot keep it flying.[50] Now wide awake, Petka asks Chapaev if he could command 'an army', 'a Front', 'all the armed forces of the Republic.' 'I can', says Chapaev, though he'd need to do a bit of studying before taking on the last of these tasks.[51] Emboldened, Petka asks a fourth question. Could Chapaev manage on a 'world scale'? At this point, even Chapaev is chastened, deflated by a consciousness of his lack of education, a frustration that pursues him throughout both book and film: 'No... I couldn't. I don't know languages!' Exasperated, he tells Petia to go to sleep and returns to his map.

Preparing for battle
There are no scenes of battle in the first half of the film. It has been used rather to establish character and relationships, with a large

number of the scenes consisting of conversations between two characters, Chapaev and Petka, Chapaev and Furmanov, Petka and Anna, Borozdin and Potapov. By contrast, in the second half of the film there are two lengthy sequences of fighting, the 'psychic attack' by General Kappel's troops and the final showdown at Lbishchensk.

To the sound of martial music, Chapaev, seen on horseback in the middle distance, looks out through binoculars from his position high on an outcrop. He announces that he expects the attack to start in half an hour. In this dramatically posed shot he wears his trademark Caucasian fur hat and a large, flowing black felt cloak [*burka*] which adds to his imposing presence.[52] Around him are Petka and some of his commanders. The scene, like a number in the 'psychic attack' sequence, is reminiscent of a Western, which is not surprising, since American Westerns had been extremely popular among Soviet audiences until the drastic cuts in the importation of foreign films at the end of the 1920s, and Soviet directors were quick to learn the lessons they could provide in the engagement of audiences.[53] Learning that the commander of the cavalry squadron, Zhukov, is not in position, Chapaev says that he will shoot him and sends Petka off to find out what is going on.

In another part of the battle-field, Anna asks an old machine-gunner whether they have enough cartridges. He replies that it depends how fierce the fighting is. Potapov is now in charge of the field kitchen, accompanied by a little boy in an army uniform several sizes too large for him. The bearded peasant who had complained earlier about the Reds looting now rides up in his cart and hands over to Potapov a large sack, probably of potatoes, and tells him to cook them for the troops. Both of these men have been treated with sympathy by the Reds and both of them have then voluntarily come over to the Red cause.

Petka tells Chapaev that there is disorder (*buza*, the very word that Teresha had used to report their earlier plundering) in the cavalry squadron, and that Zhukov has been killed by his own men. Chapaev rides off alone to sort them out. A large clearing in the forest, broken up only by a couple of tall trees, is a dramatic stage for the argument about fundamentals that has broken out among the men. An old Ukrainian soldier urges that they continue to fight until the last enemy has been defeated. He is opposed by the lanky young man who led the earlier disorder, the one who had abandoned his rifle at the start of the film. This unnamed figure has appeared in several scenes of tension, and now his story will reach the conclusion which was set in motion at his first appearance. With his rifle in his hand, he stands towering above his fellows and urges them 'Lads, let's go home!' Another man

The lanky partisan suggests desertion

quickly supports his cry, for the attraction of home is infectious. But the support for him melts away as quickly as it had arisen, and mysteriously the men pull back into serried ranks, as they had done at the start of the film. A shot rings out and the lanky partisan falls dead. The unseen Chapaev has meted out summary justice.

Though he had earlier threatened to shoot looters, Chapaev's character has so far been constructed out of charm and accessibility, and he has been able to bend his men to his will through the force of his personality and his rhetoric. This is the first time in the film that Chapaev has shown harshness, even brutality. The Vasilev Brothers had originally filmed him shooting far more deserters, but, worried about audience reaction to Chapaev's sudden cruelty and about the political sensitivity of portraying a popular Soviet hero as a man of unflinching violence, they toned this scene down. Answering questions at the State Film Institute in December 1934, Sergei Vasilev said this:

Why did we throw out the episode with the cavalry squadron? For a very simple reason. It was a question of creating the image itself and the political weight of the image. The shooting of forty men by calling out every fifth man – at the time that was the politically correct approach, the necessary measure, the answer. Maybe that is how it was. But would it have been correct to give audiences such an image of Chapaev? From my point of view, no, because there are things which are stronger than us, which can turn against us. This thing could not have been part of the image of Chapaev because it would have raised him up with enormous power, above everyone's heads. This would have done what I have been speaking about: the viewer would have stopped considering him as one of us. Not everyone can shoot from a revolver with a calm conscience and say, in a calm voice: 'Petka, re-load it.'

That is precisely why we rejected our earlier version. [...] The viewer will forgive Chapaev shooting if in his eyes the shooting is justified by a whole series of things. And that is why we came up with a new version of the shooting in the squadron after it had rebelled. Overall the picture gained by it.[54]

The conflict between the lure of home and the need to go on fighting was replayed almost exactly in a scene, also set among a band of partisan fighters in a clearing in a forest, in one of the most important films of the Second World War. In Fridrikh Ermler's *No Greater Love* [She Defends the Motherland, Ona zashchishchaet rodinu, 1943] a young man, tired of fighting, tells his fellows that they should return to their villages, to 'our own roof, our own farm'. The Germans will leave them in peace, since 'they hate only Communists and Jews'. He is shot without hesitation or mercy by 'Comrade P', the kolkhoz wife and mother Praskovia Lukianova whom the tragic loss of her husband and son in the first days of the invasion has turned into a desperate avenger. Home is a dangerous temptation.[55]   When a similar scene was proposed in the mid-1960s, however, the Soviet cinematic establishment had become more squeamish about the representation of such decisive reprisal on screen. Near the start of Alexander Askoldov's Civil War film, *The Commissar* [Komissar, 1967, not released until 1988], commissioned for the fiftieth anniversary of the Revolution, the female Commissar, Vavilova, catches up with Emelin, one of her soldiers who has gone off without permission to snatch a meeting with his wife. In the original script she summarily shoots him. The State Cinema Committee demanded changes, as a result of which Emelin is not shot but handed over to a Revolutionary Tribunal.[56]

Chapaev now turns his attention to the rest of the men. His speech is calm, in contrast to the frenzy of the lanky partisan.[57]   Drawing once again on his infinite capacity to inspire, he reminds the squadron that 'the best sons of the people are laying down their lives' and insists that they must redeem their guilt in blood. Jumping on his horse he adds that he himself will ride at their head, confirming Elan's remark during the potato strategy lesson that Chapaev was always to be found at the front. Before he can set off another unseen shot rings out. His men explain that they have followed his example and 'topped' another potential deserter. 'To horse' calls Chapaev, once again the hero of a Western. Back at the field kitchen, to the sound of distant gunfire, the boy in the over-large greatcoat asks 'uncle' Potapov what people are going to their death for. 'What for?', Potapov replies, it's clear what for, 'for life', foregrounding the motif of sacrifice that will pervade the final sequences of the film.[58] Potapov himself will not be seen again.[59]

The psychic attack

The psychic attack

Furmanov rides up to the hillock on which Chapaev had been standing and he and Elan look out over the plain before them. Three rows of General Kappel's troops come into sight in the distance.

Vladimir Oskarovich Kappel was born in 1883. He served as an officer in the First World War. As a committed monarchist, he opposed both the February and the October Revolutions and joined the White forces in the Civil War. On 8 June 1918 Socialist Revolutionaries in Samara proclaimed a rival to the Moscow government, the Committee of Members of the Consituent Assembly, known in Russian as the Komuch. Kappel was put in charge of a brigade of the People's Army created by the Komuch, which initially captured the towns of Simbirsk and Kazan, but which soon succumbed to Red counter-attacks. He later served as a Lieutenant-General under Admiral Kolchak. After the Whites were defeated on the Eastern Front in January 1920, they retreated in the so called 'Ice March', during which Kappel contracted frostbite and pneumonia, leading to his death on 26 January 1920. His men carried his body east during their retreat and he was eventually buried in the Russian cemetery in the Chinese town of Kharbin in 1922. In January 2007 he was re-buried in the cemetery of the Donskoi Monastery in Moscow.[60]

In his probing article on the representation of the White forces in *Chapaev*, E.V. Volkov points out a number of disparities with the historical record. The White enemy in the film is represented as the combined forces of the Kappel division and the Urals Cossacks, but in fact they fought together only once during the Civil War. There were 'psychic attacks' only at the start of the war. Encounters between Kappel's troops and Chapaev's in 1919 were extremely rare. Kappel's troops are very unlikely to have fought in this battle, and Chapaev, who was wounded, did not take part in it.[61] There were no officer battalions in these battles, no officer regiment by 1919. The striking black uniform they wear is a Soviet myth – no one would be dressed this well and this uniformly by this stage of the Civil War, though the English general, General Knox had supplied Kappel's men with English uniforms earlier in the year.[62] But Kappel's men were renowned as the best fighters in Kolchak's army, which meant that victory over them would bring the greatest glory to Chapaev and his men, and thus they were chosen for the role of enemy in this scene.

As Kappel's men advance, the sound of birdsong is gradually drowned out by the pounding of their side-drum. Anna and the gunner who had hidden his machine gun in the river at the start of the film watch their progress intently. Suddenly the man is shot and falls to the ground. With his dying words he puts the solitary Maxim gun in her charge. Dressed uniformly in black and with bayonets raised on their backs, the officers march in unison in the phalanx formation pioneered by Philip of Macedon, the father of Alexander the Great. With their intimidating skull and crossbones standard unfurled before them, they make a striking contrast with Chapaev's ragged riflemen, who lie waiting for them to come within range. The phalanx lowers its bayonets. Though many of them fall, they just march on. Tension is increased both by the drumming and by a succession of reaction shots, which show the battle as a struggle between the Whites and the simple people, the *narod*.[63] Two of the partisans admit to a grudging admiration for the 'beauty' with which these 'intellectuals' are marching. Anna watches and waits, showing the discipline and control which mark her as one of the troops who have arrived with Furmanov. But the 'psychic' effect begins to work on another partisan, who bares his chest and begs them to shoot him. Several of Chapaev's men turn tail in terror. Elan attempts to rally them and Furmanov blocks the path of their retreat, forcing them to return to the fighting. With the lieutenant played by Georgi Vasilev at their head, the Kappelite officers break into a run and begin to shout. Suddenly we hear the sound of machine gun fire and shots rake the ground just in front of the advancing men. With the machine gun protected by a nest she has constructed out of branches, Anna is finding her range. Other partisans begin to hurl grenades. The young lieutenant falls. The Kappelites turn tail, re-group, turn again. Anna runs out of bullets. Then, from the distance, the Cossack Cavalry, the other element of the White forces, make their attack. All would be lost, but suddenly, to the sound of the music which in Westerns signifies reinforcements bringing liberation, Chapaev leads the counter-attack. On a white steed, with sabre raised and with his black felt cloak flowing in the wind, he is such an awesome and alarming sight that the Cossacks, too, turn tail.

In Furmanov's novel the attack by General Kappel's men is dealt with in a few lines and there is no mention at all of a psychic attack. This powerful, almost wordless sequence, which has earned deserved praise from many commentators on the film, is another of the Vasilev Brothers' inventions, and it is clear that they planned it with scrupulous attention to its emotional effect on audiences. As Sergei Vasilev explained:

> We wrote in the script: when the squadron appears from behind the hill, company by company to the sound of the drum… and so on and so forth. I had this staccato sound ringing in my ears, and I imagined how it might affect a person whose individual development has been weak, who has been poorly trained and is poorly armed. What kind of training did the old army have, what elements did it consist of? The drum beat is an incontrovertible sign that they have been drilled. So this led us to the direct merging of these things. It's like in the circus, when you are watching a turn (*attraktsionnyi nomer*). What was Kappel thinking of? Of the way this would affect people like a turn. The turn was accompanied by the desperate beating of a drum. This is not accidental.
>
> As for how we shot it, how we framed it, it was absolutely clear to us that the whole key to it was that on the one hand there was a mass psychic attack and on the other there were people. They are our people. […] So it became clear: not a single close-up of the Whites and only close-ups of the Reds. The whole point here is the people. What you have here is a clash of two wills, and it is important that it is resolved in our people, and not in the Whites.[64]

Vasilev recalls that the young Red Army soldiers who played the Kappelite officers had to be drilled and trained in this unfamiliar skill for four days[65], but the resulting performance so impressed Osip Mandelshtam that he made special mention of the officers' smartness and their devil may care daring in his poem 'Ot syroi prostyni govoriashchaia' ('Speaking from the damp sheet').[66] For the critic Neia Zorkaia the marching officers are 'doll-automata, mask-people', and she compares them to the ghastly masks of the Tsarist officers in Alexander Medvedkin's film *Happiness* [Schast´e, 1934, released 15 March 1935] and to the plays of Brecht.[67] A number of critics compare the 'psychic attack' to the 'Odessa steps' sequence in *The Battleship Potemkin*, reminding us that Eisenstein was the Vasilev Brothers' cinematic mentor. In both sequences a faceless killing force marches mechanically forward against an enemy who are individualised, but the differences between the two sequences are as remarkable as the points of comparison. The enemy in *Chapaev* are armed soldiers and victory is ultimately theirs. Only one of their number, the old gunner, dies, whereas numbers of the officers are slain. Though both sequences deploy virtuoso montage, the two hundred cuts of the 'Odessa Steps' contrast with only 67 in the psychic attack.[68]

Asked whether the sequence of the Cossack attack did not, in fact, require the use of close-ups, Vasilev was frank in his reply:

> That is the fault of our technology. We had only four hours to shoot it, which made it impossible to put the composition we had thought out into effect in detail. There are some mistakes. It's a strange thing about the cinema, the viewer must understand from the first second, and if he doesn't that means that you have not done what you set out to do. We did not do what we set out to do. If it had been clear that it was the Cossacks, then we would not have needed any close-ups. This is simply a mistake in the way in which we carried out our task.
>
> A second thing is that we ourselves are guilty of removing from the scene of the battle with Kappel's men something which would have brought the viewer to his feet when the scene was shown.
>
> We didn't manage to achieve this, because we weren't allowed to, but we should have.[69]

There were no such problems of recognition in the scene of Chapaev's counter-attack, since the white steed, the Caucasian fur hat and the flowing cloak were all seen as he stood on the hillock at the beginning of the sequence. V.A. Troianovsky likens the cloak to wings, and links it to the Orthodox idea that at the Battle of Kulikovo the heavenly host were on the side of the Russians.[70] Boris Vasilev describes the cloak as historically inaccurate, insisting that it would inhibit the movement of a man on horseback, but praises the film-makers for 'boldly disdaining the inaccuracy of the detail' and 'creating a fine symbol of impulse, rage and unrestrained daring', adding that 'Chapaev, riding in a flowing cloak has become the image of the Civil War itself, has become historically authentic, accurate and undoubted'.[71] This is Chapaev in his pomp, and the image is one of the most famous in the film.

Chapaev drinks tea from a saucer in the White HQ after routing their forces

An intertitle takes us to 'The Headquarters of the Kappel Brigade'. On the wall there is a poster depicting the outcome they had hoped to see from the psychic attack. As the officers' regiment march forward in unison, Chapaev flees before them, his cloak billowing in the breeze. Above them is a verse:

S nami Bog! s nami Bog!
Krasnykh davim my kak blokh!
A truslivye chapaitsy
Udiraiut vse, kak zaitsy!

God is with us! God is with us!
We are crushing the Reds like fleas!
But the cowardly Chapaevites
Are all fleeing like hares!

Chapaev is very impressed by the poster and asks Petka to take it down.
Then Anna arrives, summoned by Chapaev. Drinking tea from a
saucer, he calls her 'madame' and asks why she had taken so long to
start firing. Learning that she was waiting for her target to get closer,
he congratulates her on her bravery and tells Petka to give her the
poster as a souvenir. In the words of Marc Ferro, Anna, like Petka
before her, has now undergone her military rite of passage. By this their
relationship has been legitimated. So now when Petka puts a
congratulatory arm around her, she does not resist. He breaks a hard
boiled egg on the table and proffers it to her.[72]

Furmanov leaves
An intertitle announces that it is autumn. Petka is mending a sheepskin
jacket, a suitcase at his side. As he works, he and the unseen Chapaev
sing an old folksong:

Otets synu ne poveril,
Chto na svete est' liubov'.
Veselyi razgovor...

The father did not believe his son
That there is such a thing as love.
A merry conversation...[73]

The sad refrain continues:

Vzial syn sabliu,
Vzial on vostru,
I zarezal sam sebia. ...
Veselyi razgovor.
On zarezal sam sebia.

The son took a sabre,
A sharp sabre
And he cut his own throat.
A merry conversation...
He cut his own throat.

The doom-laden song is appropriate to the mood of the three men in the room. Furmanov, it transpires, is leaving, packing up his books into a kit bag. Petka is mending his jacket as a sign of respect. Chapaev picks up the telegram that is lying on the table, and reads, not for the first time: 'Due to an emergency, I insist upon Furmanov's immediate departure. Sedov will take over from him. Frunze.' Chapaev has taken the news as a personal insult and is prepared to accept it only because it is signed by Frunze himself. A car draws up, so Petka finishes his sewing and carries out the Commissar's luggage as Furmanov, pipe in mouth, prepares to leave. He shakes hands with the new Commissar, and is about to shake hands with Chapaev, but they fall into a brotherly embrace, after which Chapaev punches him on the arm in exasperation at this turn of events. As Furmanov is driven off, the tune of 'Black Raven' is hummed wordlessly on the soundtrack. Thus parting is rendered an omen of death. In the words of the film theorist Béla Balázs, when Furmanov leaves 'we sense a turning point in Chapaev's fate, the idea that Chapaev is being abandoned not only by the Commissar, but also by his lucky star.'[74] While Chapaev and then Petka and Anna watch and wave, the Commissar and his driver move off into the far distance. As Nikolai Tarabukin has noted:

> Furmanov's car drives straight into the depth of the frame. Here the straight line embodies the unflinching implementation of the order of the High Command, firmness in the implementation of these orders. It is not by chance that this is the only time when we see such a straight line in the film *Chapaev*. This is a way of singling out this shot among all the others.[75]

In ideological terms, now that the mission which the Party entrusted him of 'educating' Chapaev has been accomplished, Furmanov is able to leave the Division and take on new challenges. In plot terms, having performed his single function of ideological injection, and being uninteresting in all other ways, he is expendable. The Commissar also left the Division before Chapaev's death in Furmanov's novel, but he continued to tell his tale and the novel includes his reaction to Chapaev's death. The film, by contrast, will conclude with Chapaev's death and Furmanov's participation in it is now over. Audiences will feel his departure less keenly than do Chapaev and Petka. Though always represented as Chapaev's wise teacher, as someone who is ideologically more important and from whom Chapaev must learn, he has never been allowed to emulate the Commander's charisma, and it is noticeable how small a part this character will play in the film's popular success.[76]

The final encounter
In a vast, columned hall, Colonel Borozdin and a White General are in conversation. Like Chapaev before him, Borozdin pores over a map and draws up a plan of campaign. Though the Red HQ and Chapaev are in Lbishchensk, most of his troops are further down river, at Sakharnaia, with the Brigade Commander, Elan, making it possible to cut Chapaev off. The General describes this as their last chance to be done with Chapaev and to stem their retreat; behind them is the town of Gurev, where the Ural River meets the Caspian Sea. He entrusts the campaign to Borozdin, adding, as he leaves, that the Allies have put 20,000 roubles on Chapaev's head. The wily Borozdin counters that the Allies could have been more generous, 'since there is oil in Gurev'.[77]

It is night in the Reds' camp. Petka is lying at Anna's knee, resting his head against her, leading the singing of a last, sad song:

Revela buria, dozhd´ shumel.
Vo mrake molniia blistala…

The storm was raging, the rain was noisy.
Lightning flashed in the darkness.

Other fine voices join in, for there are a number of men resting here, the low roof and cramped space contrasting vividly with the lofty emptiness of the previous scene.

I bespreryvno grom gremel.
I v debriakh buria bushevala.

And the thunder thundered unceasingly,
And the storm raged in the thickets.

The lighting of Chapaev's face shows him to be deep in thought. Another man starts the second verse of the song:

Tovarishchi ego trudov,
Pobed i gromkozvuchnoi slavy…
The comrades of his labours,
Of his victories and his noisy glory…

Sedov, the new Commissar, suggests to Chapaev that they should double the sentries, since it is a dark night. Chapaev smirks and says that the Whites are in retreat, cowed by his fighting reputation. Eventually he agrees to post a few more men. The song continues:

Sredi raskinutykh shatrov
Bespechno spali sred´ dubravy...

Among the scattered tents
They slept without a care in the oak forest...

External shots show the streets of the village to be empty, the silence broken only by birdsong. As Petia sings the line 'Vy spite, slavnye geroi' ('You are sleeping, glorious heroes'), a line which continues the association of the Red forces with heroism which has run through the film, emotion moves Chapaev to loquacity. He tells Anna and Petka that they are fortunate: they are young, they will marry, they will work together. The war will come to an end and their life will be wonderful. There will be no death.[78] He pauses for breath and another verse of the song ends 'Na slavu il´ na smert´ zovushchii!' ('Calling to glory or to death'), in direct contradiction of what Chapaev has been saying. He concedes that no one wants to die, but, recalling the words of Potapov to the young boy, he describes the struggle they are engaged in as one which makes you ready to give up your life: 'Libo oni nas, libo my ikh' ('Either we'll do for them or they'll do for us.') 'Net, my ikh', says Petka: 'No, we'll do for them'. These dramatic words are followed by silence, and Chapaev urges Petka to resume the song. Now we hear the tragic resolution of its narrative:

Kuchum, prezrennyi tsar´ Sibiri,
Prokralsia tainoiu vershinoi,
I pala, groznaia v boiakh,
Ne obnazhiv mechei, druzhina.

Kuchum, the despised Tsar of Siberia,
Crept forward along a secret high path,
And the troops, who were awesome in conflict,
Fell without baring their swords.

As the song comes to an end we see numbers of men lying haloed in light, and Petka asks Anna if he is good enough to be an actor. The song that he has been singing was extremely well known to Russian audiences and was taken from folk variants of the 1822 poem 'The Death of Ermak', by the poet Konstantin Ryleev, who was one of the leaders of the Decembrist uprising against the Tsarist regime, of 14 December 1825, and was put to death on the scaffold the following year.[79] Kuchum ruled the Siberian khanate from 1563 to 1598. He resisted the Russians, stopped paying tribute and had the Russian ambassador to the khanate murdered in 1573. Ermak, a Cossack ataman, led a force against him in the early 1580s, and Kashlyk, the capital of the Siberian khanate, fell to Ermak on 26 October 1582. But

The night before the final battle

Kuchum re-grouped his forces, and on the night of 5-6 August 1585 he caught Ermak and his men in an ambush. The sentries fell asleep. The night was dark and stormy and Kuchum's horsemen managed to ride up secretly into the Cossack camp and attack them unexpectedly. Ermak and his men were defeated. Ermak himself attempted to escape by swimming the Irtysh River, but he drowned, either under the weight of his own armour or because he had been wounded.[80]

In his 1937 talk at the State Film Institute, Sergei Vasilev explained the Brothers' reasons for using this song:

The 'Song of Ermak' is associated to some degree by all Russian people with a certain heroism, bravery, with a certain tragic death of a great man, a great hero. And therefore when 'Ermak' precedes Chapaev's death, a certain association appears in the viewer. Involuntarily, whether he likes it or not, the viewer already has an aching feeling about a great man, about a doomed hero. Against this background the viewer is already prepared for the death of Chapaev.[81]

Like 'The Black Raven' before it, 'The Death of Ermak' tells a tale of heroic death, but its words model and predict the fate of Chapaev and his men with greater specificity than does the previous song. Thus through the fates of both Ermak and Ryleev himself the song places the courage and heroism of Chapaev and his men in the context of Russian narratives of bravery and noble sacrifice. But it also makes reference to Ermak's 'fatal flaw', the 'sleeping without a care' which caused his downfall. This not only prefigures what will soon happen to Chapaev, but it goes directly against both the words spoken earlier to the sentries by Furmanov and the advice proffered by Sedov.

More lyric views of the broad Ural River and the trees in the village are accompanied by the very music which played in the earlier nocturnal scene in which Petka captured his prisoner. Now Petka and Anna are sleeping in each other's arms, while all around them Chapaev and his men are sleeping the sleep of the dead. But there are also those who are not sleeping – a large force of White Cossack Cavalry is approaching the village, bringing with it a sinister armoured car, profaning the beautiful music:

And then, when their lyric theme, the one they parted to when Petka went behind enemy lines, this same theme accompanies their sleeping and the Whites' attack, it's just terrifying. This arouses indignation in the viewer, the desire to prevent it. Because the viewer knows what is going to happen. He wants to say: wake these people up. And at the same time you have their lyric song, and the Cossacks advancing and the armoured car advancing – this all happens to the background of their lyric theme […].[82]

Chapaev, it turns out, has not doubled the sentries, and the two men on guard are also deep in sleep, making it easy for two White Cossacks to kill them and signal to the horsemen that the way is clear. Chapaev's neglect of Sedov's advice, his failure fully to achieve the consciousness that Furmanov had required of him, has brought about his own downfall. This is a matter of immense significance to the overall depiction of Chapaev in the film. In the novel, Furmanov, who was not himself of course present, says that Chapaev gave instructions for the members of the cadet school to be put on duty, adding:

> Who it was who on that fateful night removed the divisional school from the guard remains a matter of amazement and surmise. Chapaev gave no one such an order.[83]

In a diary entry for 22 September, however, he gives a different version:

> There is a rumour that some woman (?) even warned them of the coming Cossack raid on their HQ. Chapai knew about this and yet he took no measures.[84]

Conscious of what such a tactical failure can do to her great grandfather's reputation, Evgeniia Chapaeva goes out of her way to deny it, insisting that:

> After Chapaev's order for the guard to be strengthened, unarmed men were given rifles from the store and they set off in line to the outskirts of Lbishchensk. At night, however, this guard was stood down, on the orders of some unknown person. The weapons were removed from them and the people were sent off to get some rest...[85]

For Iosif Dolinsky, Chapaev's tactical lapse is evidence of his 'tragic guilt' and 'the remains of his partisan carelessness', while V. Mildon sees the consequences of his failure to listen to Sedov as ideologically necessary proof that Commissars are always right.[86] But as A. Dubrovin reminds us, Chapaev's faults, his rashness and readiness to take unjustified risks are merely an extension of his positive qualities, his bravery and his martial daring.[87] For Oleg Kovalov, a film which is officially about Chapaev's re-education cannot really be so, 'because after all Chapaev perishes, even though he has spent time with Furmanov, and no re-education results from the time spent by Furmanov in Chapaev's division'. Yet this does not raise any doubt about Chapaev in audiences' minds, since 'In *Chapaev* there is only one truly charming hero – and that is Chapaev.'[88] Some of the most astute critics of the film, like Viktor Shklovsky, realise that Chapaev's popularity can only gain from this manifestation of human weakness:
> The reason that viewers like Chapaev so much is that they see their own biography in him, they believe in themselves and they smile at their own mistakes.[89]

Colonel Borozdin, who is revealed in this sequence of the film to be a master of tactics and of cunning, checks his watch and gives the signal for the attack to begin. The Cossacks ride forward waving their sabres along a road lined with noble birch trees. Shots ring out and finally Chapaev and his men are woken from their slumbers. Some dressed in their underclothes, they attempt to resist, but their rifles are no match for an armoured car. A Cossack soldier torches the thatched roofs. The bearded peasant who had brought food to the field kitchen hides in the hay on the back of a cart. It is Anna, who from the start of the film has been associated with Furmanov, who at this point takes command, telling Chapaev that they must run to the machine guns.[90] She, Chapaev and Petka set up a Maxim gun at a high window and prepare to fire it. Chapaev, like Anna before him during the psychic attack, opens fire on the advancing waves of the White enemy.[91] Petka attempts to telephone Elan in Sakharnaia, but the line has been cut. Chapaev tells Anna and Petka to ride off there for reinforcements, but Petka cannot leave his Commander. Reversing his constant refrain, he tells Anna that 'I cannot leave him. I cannot!' Anna and Petka have parted at night before. On that occasion, they shook hands and Petka walked off in search of a prisoner. This time, they embrace, before Anna rides off into the night.[92] As the Whites continue to advance, Petka returns to Chapaev's side, but the ghastly armoured car begins its inhuman hail of bullets.[93] Chapaev is shot in the arm and Petka bandages his wound, before jumping on to the roof and disabling the armoured car with grenades. At this point the Whites bring in their own machine gun and rake the room with fire. Chapaev falls to the ground. 'Ámba, Vasilii Ivanych', says Petka, 'we're done for', we have to retreat. Though the Commander retorts, in another of his plangent phrases, 'Chapaev has never retreated', he is now too weak to do other than obey Petka's orders. Thus, in this final scene, Chapaev has been reduced from leadership to following the orders of his 'children', Anna and Petka, further increasing his tragic appeal. Petka carries him out. The screen fades to black.

A breathless Anna arrives in Sakharnaia and Elan gathers his forces for the counter-attack. Back in Lbishchensk, Petka has dragged Chapaev to the edge of a high cliff over the Ural River.[94] Down below some of his men are already attempting to swim across to safety. Petka rallies others to help him carry help Chapaev down the steep slope and to the water's edge, but when they try to carry him further he shakes them off, exclaiming 'Ia sam!', I'll do it myself! While Petka continues to resist the Whites, now firing from a rifle, Chapaev seems to be making good progress across the mighty river, swimming with his one good arm, but

Photo from the set: the annihilation of the White forces

the water is being raked with bullets. 'You're lying, you won't get me', 'Vresh´, ne voz´mesh´´', he mutters to the Black Raven of death.[95] Petka runs out of bullets and is shot and killed as he attempts to enter the river. Chapaev swims on, but now the Whites attack him with machine-gun fire. To the sound of what Sergei Vasilev called Popov's 'funeral march' his head disappears beneath the waters.[96] Even in the manner of his death Chapaev emulates Ermak. The shot cuts to a scene of the broad, meandering river, the last of the beautiful scenes of Russian nature which punctuate the film.[97] To music like that of a Western, Elan, Anna and two other horsemen lead the counter-attack. Elan has gathered a vast and intimidating force and the Cossacks flee in disarray.[98] The bearded peasant cuts down Borozdin while he is saddling his horse and attempting to flee.[99] The remains of the White forces retreat to the cliff face, which is blown away by Elan in the last, ecstatic shot of the film.

The film's double ending amply satisfies audiences with both death and transcendence, both heroic tragedy and righteous vengeance. In this context it is fascinating to be reminded that the Brothers had experimented with other endings. Both the 'literary script' published in the journal *Literaturnyi sovremennik* in September 1933 and an early version of the 'directors' script' ended with a scene set in liberated Lbishchensk, in which Anna and Petka (who had survived his shooting) were present at a ceremony which included solemn speeches and funeral marches at the burial mound of the fallen. To the sound of Chapaev's words about the happy future the forces of the contemporary Soviet Army appear, with tanks, armoured cars and planes. This version was abandoned before being shot as out of keeping with the mood of the film.[100] Instead the Brothers wrote an epilogue, set at the time of the film's making, which fulfilled the prophecy Chapaev had made for them. This is how the scene is described by Dolinsky in his study of the film:

> In this version Petka was only wounded that last tragic morning on the bank of the Ural. He escaped from the Cossacks… Thirteen or fourteen years have passed. Anna and Petka have a son. Anna occupies an important post in industry. Petka is a Regimental Commander. We catch up with them in summer in a remarkable garden in flower.[101]

Pisarevsky gives even more detail, setting the scene in an apple orchard in which Anna and Petka are playing with their children. The sequence was actually shot in a garden in Gori, in Georgia and Pisarevsky publishes a remarkable photograph of a happy Anna and Petka joyously picking apples, but it too was rejected as at odds with the overall structure of the film.[102] The traditional preference of Russian audiences for sad endings prevailed.

4. Reception. Chapaev's extraordinary afterlife

Stalin watches the film

Chapaev was completed on 22 October 1934 and passed with minor changes by the State Cinema Directorate on 2 November. It was shown to Stalin on the evening of 4 November, in one of his regular Kremlin screenings. Boris Shumiatsky, the Head of Soiuzkino, and therefore the man with overall charge of the Soviet film industry, was responsible for supplying the films to be shown, and he kept detailed notes on the reactions of Stalin and his Politburo colleagues.[1] At his first viewing Stalin found some of the initial scenes confusing, but as soon as Chapaev asked 'What does the Commissar think?' he began to warm to the film, noting, approvingly, 'He's testing him.' More and more positive comments followed, and when the film was over, he turned to Shumiatsky and said:

> You can be congratulated on your success. It has been done well, wisely and tactfully. Chapaev is good and so are Furmanov and Petka. The film will have great educational significance. It is a good present for the holiday.[2]

After this the Vasilev Brothers were presented to Stalin, and he and the other Politburo members with whom he had watched the film congratulated them on their brilliant and truthful work, predicting that it would be a well earned success.

Stalin watched the film three more times on 7 and 8 November, in the company of Kaganovich, Voroshilov, Molotov and Zhdanov, who all, perhaps unsurprisingly, greatly admired the film, and singled out for praise exactly the aspects such as 'What does the Commissar think?' which had previously been praised by Stalin.[3] On the night of 10-11 November 1934 he watched the film twice, this time in the company of Molotov, Zhdanov, the Soviet President, Mikhail Kalinin, and Sergei Kirov, the Leningrad Party chief, and asked about the early press reaction. Learning that Kirov had not yet seen the film, he teasingly reproved him for not paying sufficient attention to the development of Soviet cinema, even though *Chapaev*, like several of the most important recent Soviet films, had been made at the Lenfilm studios.[4] On 15 November during his ninth viewing, he complained that with only between 400 and 500 screens equipped to show sound films, around 2,000 regions of the Soviet Union were still unable to see such films. On 20 November, during his eleventh viewing, he

Advertising still for the film

asked again about press reaction and suggested that it was time that *Pravda* ran a leader, summing up reaction so far.[5] And Stalin continued to watch the film, during December 1934 and on into 1935. On 2 April 1935 he watched the new silent version, in a group that included his children Svetlana and Vasili, but found it to be over-long. By 10 November 1935, when the film had been out for a year, Stalin had seen it 27 times. Four months later, on 9 March 1936, he watched it for the 38th time and told Ordzhonikidze that it was 'of course, the best film'.[6] In fact the aspects of the film which he praised had hardly changed since his first viewing – on 10 November 1935, during his 27th viewing, for example, he singled out 'the plot, the acting, the extreme simplicity and clarity in which the epoch and its people are shown.'[7] Another reason for his liking the film may, of course, have been that its hero was safely dead, unlike other Civil War heroes whose current behaviour was arousing his suspicion. Some of Chapaev's fighters who survived the Civil War would indeed fall victim to the purges in the coming years, notably Ivan Kutiakov, the prototype of the character of Elan in the film, and Chapaev's replacement as Commander of the Division. Popular awareness that this could be the fate of former heroes is provided in the memoirs of Evgeniia Ginzburg. When the arrested former teacher and journalist was being transported to a Siberian labour camp in July 1939, she heard a rumour circulating that 'Anka, Chapaev's machine gunner' was also on the prison train.[8] Further graphic evidence of these losses is provided by David King, who included two versions of a photograph taken on 9 June 1919 of Chapaev and his fellow fighters in the Urals in his book *The Commissar Vanishes*. The version of the photograph published in 1926 and 1932 contains 41 men, but in a later form the same photograph has only 30 men in it and four of the faces of those who have been removed have been superimposed upon those who are left.[9] The story of the Civil War was being re-written. In the words of Konstantin Simonov:

> In his time Stalin first supported Chapaev, and then advanced the idea for a film about Shchors. Both Chapaev and Shchors were authentic heroes of the Civil War, but overall they were figures of the second rank. Stalin's support of Chapaev and his idea about a film about Shchors came about when first rank figures, who occupied important posts in the contemporary army, men such as Egorov, Tukhachevsky and Uborevich, who commanded the South-Western, Western and Far-Eastern fronts, were destined to disappear from the history of the Civil War - not just to disappear from life, but to disappear from history.[10]

The same point is made by the critic Evgeni Gromov, who says of the film:

> It answered both to Stalin's political and ideological interests and to his personal artistic tastes.
> From the end of the 20s the General Secretary, who had destroyed the Party opposition, made a planned attempt to 'correct' the history of the Civil War, the heroes of which often had the reputation of being former comrades-in-arms of Trotsky, or simply military men

whom the Boss found disagreeable. Vasili Chapaev belonged to neither of these groups. He was a relatively neutral figure, and not a figure of the first rank. He fought honourably and bravely, even though they say that in life he was a harsh and even cruel man, something which could not trouble the General Secretary, and besides, the film did not touch upon this subject. It was only the enemies who were shown as cruel.[11]

The initial reception in the Soviet press

The first extensive printed engagement with the film was in a review by Sergei Dinamov carried in *Pravda* on 3 November. It opened by describing the tension evoked by the scene of the psychic attack, which it compared to the Odessa Steps sequence in *The Battleship Potemkin*, and called 'one of the best scenes in world cinema'. More lavish praise followed and the piece concluded by saying that people should follow the Vasilev Brothers' example and make films which 'educate heroes, infect people with courage and summon them fierily to struggle for socialist revolution'. Dinamov's single adverse criticism was of the acting of Boris Blinov in the part of Furmanov, which he found 'too soft' and betraying 'a certain enfeeblement'.[12]

Izvestiia first considered the film in a review by the leading critic Khrisanf Khersonsky on 10 November. In Khersonsky's view *Chapaev* was historically and psychologically truthful, the portrait of Chapaev himself was lifelike and comprehensible, the Civil War was shown optimistically almost for the first time in Soviet cinema, and Illarion Pevtsov was magnificent in the role of the White Colonel, Borozdin. But he ended his short notice with 'special regret' that for all the 'authenticity' and 'ideological maturity' of the film, Furmanov, 'the representative of the party that was educating the Chapaevs', was shown 'very uncertainly, incompletely and superficially'.[13] Khersonsky had offered measured praise for what he took to be a run of the mill film, and he must have been amazed by the torrent of criticism that his review provoked.

Khersonsky and *Izvestiia* had neglected to ascertain the opinion of the Soviet Union's leading film fan before printing their cool assessment of *Chapaev*. Now they were to pay the price. For on the evening of 10 November, the day on which Khersonsky's review appeared, Stalin asked Shumiatsky about press reaction, only to be told that Izvestiia had 'diluted its barrel of honeyed praise with a spoonful of tar', by asking for a strengthening of the role of the Commissar. When this interpretation was confirmed by Molotov, Stalin replied:

Oh, these critics. Such things are not written without purpose. They disorientate people. [..] Mekhlis will have to get firmly to the bottom of this case.[14]

Lev Mekhlis was the editor of *Pravda*. According to Shumiatsky, Stalin then phoned Mekhlis and arranged for *Pravda* to publish an article 'giving a correct orientation in this question.' He continued:

The critics also need to be taught to write correct, and not obviously incorrect, things, especially about such an exceptionally talented and enormously tactfully made film.[15]

On 12 November *Pravda* duly published an article under the by-line 'cinemagoer', entitled 'Little pictures in the paper and big pictures on screen. About Khris. Khersonsky's film review in *Izvestiia*', in which lavish praise of the film is interwoven with repeated attacks on Khersonsky. In the opinion of 'cinemagoer', *Chapaev* is 'a real event in Soviet cinema, its pride, its fine present to the viewer'.

The film *Chapaev* is real, moving life. You forget that you are just a viewer, you forget that what is before you is the past. You forget because the film is so gripping and so involving that the viewer turns into an active participant in events.

Khersonsky's review, by contrast, was attacked as 'grey, bureaucratically dry and professionally boring' and as a 'typical example of an indifferent, inert, peevishly bureaucratic attitude to one's duties'.[16] The polemic between the two newspapers over Khersonsky's review would develop into a broader argument over Soviet cinema in general, and is also clearly part of a struggle for influence between them. If Mekhlis, the editor of *Pravda*, was a loyal Stalin ally, then Nikolai Bukharin, who edited *Izvestiia* from 1934 to January 1937, and attracted a number of leading writers to work on the paper, was highly distrusted by Stalin. He would be arrested in February 1938 and executed in March 1938

On 15 November *Izvestiia* felt obliged to return to the film at greater length, with a longer article, entitled 'A remarkable achievement', and a poem by Elena Ryvina, 'Watching Chapaev'.[17] The poem is about the experience of watching the film in a Leningrad cinema, and describes wiping 'the best tear, a real tear' from 'disobedient eyes' at the end of the film. It concludes by wishing that Chapaev had survived so that he too could have watched the film. The article, which is unsigned, and therefore must be taken to represent the view of the paper's editorial board, is considerably more fulsome than Khersonsky's earlier notice. It describes the film as full of unforgettable and stunning imagery and goes out of its way to stress that 'the powerful disciplinary and ideological influence of the Party and its revolutionary intellect, which is embodied on screen in the figure of the Commissar, Furmanov, is shown in stirring and restrained tones', before concluding:

> Everyone, everyone, everyone must see this production and experience that sense of pride which appears when you watch this remarkable artistic achievement.

But in an extended postscript, the article complains that *Pravda* has devoted so much space to Khersonsky's review, which, though 'pale and weak', was only a 'preliminary note about the film'; and besides, Sergei Dinamov had been even more negative about the portrayal of Furmanov in his notice in *Pravda* of 3 November 1934.

Izvestiia's partial apology did not satisfy *Pravda*, which returned to the fray the following day, suggesting that Dinamov's remarks had been taken out of context, and concluding, with heavy sarcasm, that from now on readers of *Izvestiia* should treat all film reviews as merely 'preliminary notes'.[18] But with both *Izvestiia* and *Pravda* now singing the film's praises, the official critical line on *Chapaev* was abundantly clear. Attacks on Khersonsky continued, and eventually, on 8 March 1935, he wrote a 'letter to the editors' of the film journal *Kino*, in which he re-iterated that his review had been written in very compressed form at the request of the *Izvestiia* editorial board, who themselves had cut it further before publication. Nevertheless he conceded that he had been mistaken in not 'illuminating the merits of this fine Soviet film more convincingly', and thanked *Pravda* for giving a correct political and artistic assessment of the film and putting a stop to the phenomenon of 'us critics' paying insufficient attention to the best works of Soviet cinema. The letter was not published until 22 March 1935, and it did not get Khersonsky off the hook. The editors of *Kino* followed his letter with their own reply, in which they condemned him for waiting so long to respond to just criticism, and further accused him of 'clearly not having fully absorbed' *Pravda's* lesson, since he still failed to confess his error frankly, preferring to blame the *Izvestiia* editorial board.[19]

Even then the polemic was not over. Four days later, complaining in a front page article about *Izvestiia's* coverage of the recently completed Moscow Film Festival, Pravda reminded its readers of the 'shameful failure of the paper in assessing the most remarkable artistic document of our epoch, the film *Chapaev'* and its subsequent enforced change of position, as evidence that its rival paper had 'no luck' with matters of cinema.[20]

By the middle of November 1934 other critics and other papers were also writing about the film, though it is remarkable how similar their views were to the official line. The issue of the journal *Kino* for 16 November contained 12 reports and articles on the film over two full pages.[21] One of the contributors, the critic Boris Alpers, found it to be magnificent, emotionally charged and dynamic, and considered the image of Chapaev to be one of the greatest achievements of Soviet cinema. While acknowledging the difficulty of the role of Furmanov, which risked becoming boring and didactic, he insisted that Boris Blinov brought liveliness and passion to the part, and displayed the charisma which Furmanov had in life. He singled out the scene of the psychic attack as a sign of the strength of the White enemy, and considered that the decision not to caricature the Whites, but to show them as 'wise, strong people, military professionals' only increased audience admiration for Chapaev's achievements.[22] Two days later *Literaturnaia gazeta*, the organ of the Union of Soviet Writers, carried a cartoon and a leader proclaiming the victory of *Chapaev* over *The Happy Guys,* the musical directed by Grigori Alexandrov which would have its delayed release in December, and an article 'At last!', by Sergei Eisenstein, who had been the patron of the Vasilev brothers earlier in their career. In a rather abstruse analysis of the 'stages' of Soviet film, Eisenstein found in *Chapaev* a 'brilliant gallery of heroic individuals', which could count Shakespeare's history plays among its antecedents, and an unforgettable picture of the period.[23]

On 20 November *Pravda* devoted an entire page to the film under the title 'A film about great exploits, about valour, about glory: *Pravda's* questionnaire among the viewers of *Chapaev'*. Of the eighteen short pieces published here, thirteen are viewer responses. Students and a professor, workers and a Hero of the Soviet Union are unanimous in their praise of the film, which they find gripping from the very start, and almost unbearably moving at the end. A worker from a State Farm in the Leningrad region had wanted to jump on to the White soldier who shot *Chapaev* and suffocate him, but instead left the cinema determined to put even more passion into his work. The writer Lev Nikulin speaks of emerging from the cinema on to Arbat Square in Moscow and seeing 'living Chapaevs', serving in the Red Army and building the new metro. Veterans of the Civil War, some of whom had fought with Chapaev himself, find it historically accurate and a useful lesson for the present day. Under the headline

'Millions are going to watch *Chapaev*', there are four updates on the film's success. It is reported that work is about to start on a silent version of the film, to make sure that it can be shown in places not yet equipped for showing sound films; that in the first 10 days of exhibition in Moscow and Leningrad, 1,200,000 people have seen the film; that 80 copies have been printed instead of the usual 40 or 50 and that copies have been sent to Paris and New York; and that other copies have been sent to the army divisions who worked as extras on the film. In the central piece on the page, printed between portraits of Babochkin and Blinov, the Vasilev Brothers report 'How we worked on *Chapaev*', insisting that:

> We consider that the success of our film is not a matter of chance. It is a natural consequence of the general growth of our film industry under the leadership of the Party and its leader, Comrade Stalin.[24]

If on 20 November *Pravda* was confident that 'Millions are going to watch *Chapaev*', by the next day, in a front page leader, it was certain that 'The whole country will watch *Chapaev*'. This was the first time the paper had devoted an editorial to a single film, and an unprecedented act of ideological marketing. The change from the imperfective future ('budut smotret'') of the previous day to the perfective future ('"Chapaeva" posmotrit vsia strana'), even suggested an element of coercion and threat.[25] In the words of the article:

> *Chapaev* is an enormous event in the history of Soviet art. *Chapaev* invisibly and powerfully multiplies the link between the Party and the mass. A work of art of great quality, *Chapaev* convincingly and eloquently demonstrates the organising role of the Party. *Chapaev* shows how the Party tames the elements and moves them along the paths of Revolution and victories. [...]
> The Party has received a new and powerful means of educating the class consciousness of the young. The young see the enemy in person and hate him more strongly. Their hatred for the enemy, combined with a rapturous admiration for the heroic memory of the fighters who fell for the Revolution, acquires the same strength as their passionate love for their socialist motherland. The whole country will watch the film. Hundreds of copies will be made for the sound screen. And silent versions will be made too, so as to show *Chapaev* in all corners of our vast country – in towns, villages, collective farms, settlements, in barracks, in clubs and in squares.[26]

The leader concludes by suggesting that watching the film will convince viewers that 'a new world has been created':

> We have our great Red Army, ready to defend the world of great socialist construction. And if at some point an enemy tries to poke its nose in, our socialist motherland has at its disposal an abundance both of material resources and of the highest moral strength to rout and destroy the enemy.[27]

The following day the same title, 'The whole country will watch *Chapaev*', headed a report on progress in bringing this prophecy to pass. The Leningrad film processing factory was now devoting its entire production to *Chapaev*, working three shifts, 24 hours a day. Sixty copies were already in circulation, ten of them being shown in sixteen Moscow cinemas. Five further copies were being shown in Leningrad, and three in Rostov-on-Don, Novorossiisk and Ivanovo, the town from which Furmanov had led the volunteer weavers to join Chapaev. Other copies had been sent to the army and the navy. Over 30 copies had been sent to the other republics of the Soviet Union. The situation was considerably less bright in the countryside, where so far there were only about twenty sound screens out of a total of 28,000 venues for showing films. The need to show *Chapaev* in the countryside would motivate an increase in their number. The article concluded by reporting that in the fifteen days since its release *Chapaev* had now been seen by more than four million viewers.[28] On the same day, in *Izvestiia*, the writer Lev Kassil reported on the phenomenon of people going back to see the film for a second and third time, so as to see Chapaev alive again, before concluding that the film had raised the culture of Soviet cinema to a new level and that politically and ideologically it 'profoundly and convincingly develops the theme of elemental heroism headed by the Party's will'.[29] Also on 22 November, the front page of *Kino* carried a Resolution of the Presidium of the Central Committee of Kino-Photo Workers about *Chapaev*, which demanded that film workers be made to study the film and also announced that the directors, the cameramen, Sigaev and Ksenofontov, and the production designer, Makhlis, were all going to be offered 'free trips to the best sanatoria'.[30]

The following day *Izvestiia* reported that *Chapaev* had now been seen in Moscow alone by 800,000 people, and that the 10 copies supplied so far to Moscow were now being ferried around *eighteen* Moscow cinemas.[31] The politically educational role of the film was also stressed in a letter to *Leningradskaia pravda* from A. Tiutin, the secretary of the Party Committee of the *Red Putilovets* factory:

This real, Party, Bolshevik work of art, this film connects with our contemporary life. In our days heroes like Chapaev, Petka and Anna are models in the struggle for socialism, rise to the heights of the stratosphere, sail in the harsh waters of the Arctic.

Chapaev is of enormous help for us Party workers. Its educational and organisational role is colossal.[32]

The same sentiment was expressed the following day in the leading article in *Komsomolskaia pravda*, written by Kliment Voroshilov, the People's Commissar for Military and Navy Affairs, who described *Chapaev* as 'an exceptionally interesting film... the best representation of the Civil War. This is where our young people can study.'[33]

Further corroboration of this sentiment was provided in the same issue of the paper by a letter from a young woman worker, A. Baranova, in which she described how watching the film had made her feel as if she was directly taking part in the events it portrayed.[34]

And still the stream of laudatory articles continued. On 26 November 1934, under the heading 'A Hero', *Pravda* carried a new appreciation of Furmanov's novel and a letter to the Vasilev brothers from A. Orlova, a former Red Army machine-gunner, who had been particularly struck by the episode of the psychic attack, which recalled her own very similar experiences.[35] The next day *Krasnaia zvezda* carried a report of the reaction to the film among young soldiers. When the commissar of the first regiment of the Moscow Division of Proletarian Fusiliers asked his men what lessons could be learnt from watching *Chapaev*, one of them, Medvedev, replied that he had been struck especially by the psychic attack, since it showed him clearly that the Red Army had been up against a strong enemy, and reminded him that they should expect just such violent attacks in the near future.[36] On 29 November the Brothers promised in *Izvestiia* to consider all the comments they had heard at screenings of the film when working on future projects,[37] and on the following day the paper carried a report of the 'unanimous' praise of the film at an evening at the House of the Soviet Writer.[38] The year ended with Voroshilov signing a decree awarding gold watches to the Brothers, to Boris Babochkin and to the composer, Gavriil Popov.[39]

Broader recognition

An All-Union Creative Conference of Workers in Soviet Cinema was held from 8-13 January 1935 and on 11 January an award ceremony was held at the Bolshoi Theatre in belated commemoration of the fifteenth anniversary of the nationalisation of the cinema industry in

August 1919. The Vasilev Brothers received the Order of Lenin, while Babochkin was made a People's Artist of the USSR and Blinov, Kmit, Miasnikova, and Shkurat were all made Honoured Artists of the Republic.[40] That same day, *Pravda* devoted its first three pages, half the issue, to the achievements of the Soviet film industry. The lead publication was anniversary congratulations from Stalin to Soviet Cinema, in which he mentioned but one film by name, announcing that the Soviet authorities were waiting for 'new films, which, like *Chapaev*, will glorify the greatness of the historic deeds in the struggle for workers' and peasants' power in the Soviet Union...'. The film is again singled out in a greeting to the industry from the Soviet of People's Commissars, for 'pointing the way to new and greater successes for Soviet cinema', and in another piece calling for 'More Vivid Pictures.'[41] On the following page, in a long article about Soviet cinema anticipating his book on the subject, which would appear later in the year, Boris Shumiatsky described *Chapaev* as resulting from the 'stubborn struggle for Socialist realism' and as 'indissolubly connected to the general uplift in Soviet cinema', while Vsevolod Pudovkin hymned the film's 'unprecedented success' noting that 'the victory of the Vasilev Brothers is also my victory, and the victory of everyone working in Soviet cinema'.[42]

Much of the discussion at the Conference was devoted to the *Chapaev* model, which elicited lavish praise from the Brothers' fellow film makers. Alexander Dovzhenko, who had told the critic Viktor Shklovsky that he intended to 'put another diamond in the crown which has been placed on *Chapaev*', spoke with characteristic emotion:

> We have seen lots and lots of horsemen in films, starting with William Hart. But nothing happened to the thousands, the hundreds of thousands of viewers. But when Chapaev flew out from behind a hill in his cloak and on his grey horse, with a sword, which had been placed in his hands by the Communist Party and the social revolution, the country burst into applause, and even Eisenstein forgot whether Chapaev was cutting down the enemy in long shot, medium shot or close-up.

> [...] And the country burst into applause. And so it is not interesting whether there is or is not continuity between *Chapaev* and *Battleship Potemkin*. Something else is interesting here. What is interesting is where our cinema should draw its strength from, where it should draw its themes. We should study the popular, revolutionary epos.[43]

Leonid Trauberg, who with Grigori Kozintsev had just directed *The Youth of Maxim*, praised the film for its overall picture of the epoch, for depicting a 'downgraded' hero, whom viewers could feel equal to, and for the film-makers' careful preparation through the study of historical materials, and discussions with participants in the events. He did also offer one piece of negative criticism: he felt that the the portrayal of the class enemy was ineffective, 'because of lapses of taste and stylistic errors in the cinematography'.[44]

The following month *Chapaev* was the opening film at the First Moscow International Film Festival, which ran from 21 February to 2 March 1935. The playwright Nikolai Pogodin, who was present at the screening of the film to foreign guests, recalls his nervousness that it would flop, especially since the translation of the dialogue was indequate. Initially the audience seemed indifferent, but at the scene of the psychic attack they burst into applause, only to stop suddenly for fear that they would be seen to be applauding the Whites.[45] The film was a success, and First Prize at the Festival was awarded to the Lenfim studio, for *Chapaev* and the other films it was showing. In a book about the achievements of Soviet cinema published in English to accompany the festival, the playwright Vladimir Kirshon found the film contained 'a Bolshevik passion', while Furmanov's widow considered it 'true both historically and artistically' and Chapaev's son called it a 'historical document of our epoch from which we, the young commanders of the Red Army, shall get our education'.[46] The same point was made by Marshal Tukhachevsky in a collection of articles devoted to the film: 'The film Chapaev mobilises the viewer to vigilance in the struggle against the enemy, who exploits any carelessness, any yawning on our part'.[47]

By now more extensive attempts were being made to explain the film's phenomenal success. The critic Osip Brik suggested that it proved that contemporary viewers had not tired of socio-political films and did not want only 'lyrical, every day, light films, based on love and laughter'. He considered the film's achievement to be in treating an engaging political theme with great technical mastery, mastery which he ascribed to the 'remarkable schooling in film art' they had undergone when editing foreign films.[48] Viktor Shklovsky, a critic who, like Brik, had emerged from the Formalist movement, took a more nuanced line. He complained that the film was:

> [...] made with mistakes, with careless studio work, where the columns are badly made and there was clearly not enough money for the set design, with too few extras, who rush around the woods

trying to give the impression of being large masses of people, although of course there are no woods in the Ural steppe outside Lbishchensk.

Nevertheless, Shklovsky concluded that 'in *Chapaev* the most profound essence of art has changed'.[49] Iuri Olesha called it 'the vanguard of our art', compared the achievements of contemporary Soviet film makers to those of Renaissance painters, and complained that film critics were incapable of adequately assessing their achievements.[50] For Maxim Gorky the film's secret lay in its 'happy combination of wonderful material and a correct approach to it by the directors, who know the laws of art'. He praised the constant dynamism of the hero, and the film's compelling sense of conflict, since 'the soul of a work of art always has been and will be conflict', before concluding:

> Yes, their picture will live like a great and eternally living popular epic. It is full of enormous social breath. That is why its artistic significance is not transient.[51]

For Boris Shumiatsky, in his book proposing a model for Soviet cinema, *Kinematografiia millionov* [A Cinema for the Millions], *Chapaev* is 'the best film produced by Soviet cinema in the whole period of its existence', the 'real summit of film art', distinguished by '*exceptional* simplicity' and '*vital truth*'. Chapaev himself is 'drawn in rich and vivid colours' but 'not embellished'. Furthermore 'there is nothing superfluous' in the film which has 'few words but many ideas'. The film has shown that 'the decisive factors in a dramatic work are the *characters*, the profundity of the subject and the breadth of ideas'. Overall he considers that 'the whole film in its entirety sustains a dynamic pace that corresponds to the style of socialist realism and to the very essence of cinema', though he does consider certain scenes, including the playing of the Moonlight Sonata, the songs before the final battle and Furmanov's departure to be 'drawn out', reducing the pace of the action.[52]

But perhaps the most remarkable response to *Chapaev* in the year after its release was by the poet Osip Mandelshtam. Mandelshtam saw the film in his Voronezh exile in April 1935, while his wife, Nadezhda, was away in Moscow. Though only two poems inspired by the film survive, the memoirs of Emma Gershtein suggest that he may originally have written others, which were then destroyed by his wife, who resisted his enthusiasm:

Then she tore up the drafts of two poems in which you could sense
enthusiasm, yes, the enthusiasm of an artist who had seen sound
cinema as if for the first time [...] and, what is most important, his
struggle, the vacillation and wounded state of his   consciousness
since he had shown himself to be an opponent of the enormous
sense of uplift with which the directors, the Vasilev Brothers, had
managed to infect him through the film *Chapaev.*[53]

The first of the surviving poems 'Ot syroi prostyni govoriashchaia'
('Talking out of a damp sheet', April - June 1935) directly evokes the
impression of seeing the film:

> Nadvigalas´ kartina zvuchashchaia
> Na menia, i na vsekh, i na vas...

> The sound film was moving
> Towards me, towards everyone, towards you...

It concludes with precisely the desire to be re-made, *re-patterned* into
the shape of the new regime which had so alarmed his wife:

> Izmeriai menia, krai, perekraivai –
> Chuden zhar prikreplennoi zemli! –
> Zakhlestnulas´ vintovka Chapaeva:
> Pomogi, razviazhi, razdeli!..

> Measure me, my land, repattern me
> How miraculous is the heat of attached earth!
> Chapaev's rifle choked and sank
> Help me, untie the knot, pass a fair judgment![54]

The second poem 'Den´ stoial o piati golovakh' ('It was a Five-Headed
Day', April-May 1935) connects his impressions of the film to his
memory of the train journey to his initial place of exile, Cherdyn, on
the upper reaches of the Kama river in the Urals, closer to the area
where *Chapaev* is set. It ends with the certainty that Chapaev, though
drowned, will rise again, a motif that recurs in the reception of the
film, justified both by the fact that his dead body is never seen and as
a metaphor for viewers' enthusiasm.

> Poezd shel na Ural. V raskrytye rty nam
> Govoriashchii Chapaev s kartiny skakal zvukovoi...

Za brevenchatym tylom, na lente prostynnoi
Utonut´ i vskochit´ na konia svoego!

The train was going to the Urals. Into our open mouths
The talking Chapaev was galloping from a sound film –
Behind a log fence, on a bedsheet tape –
To drown and to spring back on your horse![55]

Popular affection
The huge popular appeal of *Chapaev* was manifested in all sorts of
ways. On 11 January 1935, Vsevolod Pudovkin had written of seeing
two boys leaving the cinema. One was crying, because he felt sorry
for Chapaev. The other, who had been watching the film for the
fourth time, assured him that you got used to it. Back in the cinema,
audiences who had seen it even more times were speaking the lines
before the characters, while in the street a policeman quoted
Chapaev's words when reprimanding a driver, confident that he
would be understood.[56] In a book published later in the year about
the construction of the Moscow underground system, I.D.
Gotseridze, who was in charge of work digging one of the shafts,
recalled that 'more than once in difficult moments working on the
metro I recalled the image of Chapaev, who was utterly devoted to
his cause, who was courageous and who could make the masses
follow in his wake'.[57]

According to Dmitri Pisarevsky, *Chapaev* was seen by over
30,000,000 people in the year following its release.[58] Just over three
years later, in an article stressing the 'important role played by the
cinema among the ideological means of communist education',
Semen Dukelsky, who had been placed in charge of the State
Committee for Cinematographic Affairs in March of the previous
year, reported that the film had by then attracted 50,000,000 viewers.[59]
Though the critic Neia Zorkaia contends that the figures which
appeared in central newspapers suggesting that 'thousands, tens of
thousands of additional viewers' had seen the film were 'absolutely
arbitrary', she also concedes that 'in this case the metaphor was
probably in accordance with the truth: yes, everyone watched
Chapaev'.[60] Seventy two copies had been struck from the negative in a
very short time, and by late 1935 it had begun to deteriorate so badly
that measures had to be taken. The negative was send abroad for
repair, and on its return the Organisational Bureau of the Central
Committee of the Communist Party passed a resolution, in December
1935, establishing an archive of film negatives, in which documentary

materials showing Lenin and Stalin as well as several important films were to be held. Most important of all was *Chapaev*, which was to be held 'in a special safe in the Main Directorate for the Cinematic and Photographic Industry under the personal responsibility of Comrade Shumiatsky, without whose permission no one must have access to the negative.' Thus the success of *Chapaev* led to a major step in the establishment of Gosfilmofond, the Soviet State film archive.[61]

It was very soon and very widely recorded that phrases from the film had entered the language,[62] and that children were playing at Chapaev and Petka. An anecdote circulated about a young boy who kept watching the film showing after showing, never leaving the cinema. Ask why he didn't go home he replied 'I'm waiting'. Asked what he was waiting for he replied: 'Maybe this time he'll get across'. In another anecdote on the same lines a group of boys run from cinema to cinema and ask:

Are you showing *Chapaev*?
Yes.
Does he drown?
Yes.
That means it's not here. Come on, lads, somewhere there's a cinema where he doesn't drown.[63]

In a series of pieces published in *Pravda* on 5 September 1939 to mark the twentieth anniversary of Chapaev's death, it was stated that Soviet children were raised on tales of Chapaev's exploits, and that such contemporary heroes as the pilot Valeri Chkalov and the polar explorer Ivan Papanin were part of 'Chapaev's great family of heroes'.[64] The boy hero of the children's film *The Patriot* [Patriot], directed by Ian Frid, which was released at the end of that year, runs away from home to become a border guard. When a group of Young Pioneers decide that he is a spy and give chase, he emulates Chapaev by swimming away across a river with the words: 'You're lying, you won't get me.'

The success of the film also inspired new songs and popular tales about Chapaev, in many of which he survived to continue the fight against the Whites.[65] The famous captain of the Moscow Spartak football team, Nikolai Starostin, became known as Chapai by his fellow players because of his propensity to take command and because he waved his arms about so much when giving them instructions.[66] And in a speech delivered on 15 March 1936 to mark the tenth anniversary of the death of Furmanov, the writer Isaak

Babel, who had been involved in early attempts to film the novel, pondering the reasons for the phenomenal success of a film in which both direction and acting were not beyond reproach, concluded rhetorically that the film 'wrung our hearts' because it had been made not in a film studio but 'by the whole country'.[67]

The late 1930s
The film's reputation was further cemented by the appearance in 1936 of *Chapaev. O fil'me* [Chapaev. About the Film], a book which combined biographical material about Chapaev, memoirs of work on the production, and extensive critical analysis.[68] It did attract some unusually adverse criticism at the beginning of 1938, when Boris Shumiatsky was dismissed from his post as Head of Soiuzkino and arrested. The following month, the leading film journal, Iskusstvo kino, carried an editorial 'The Fascist cur eradicated'.[69] The very close association of Shumiatsky with the Chapaev cult probably motivated the appearance in the next issue of the magazine of an article by Mikhail Shneider which, while praising the film's 'national elements', attacked the love story between Anna and Petka as a tribute to a 'faceless, international plot cuisine, spiced with genrisme and scenes from everyday life' and as 'a hack quotation of Americanism'.[70] But Chapaev's reputation was too solid, and its backers too important, for it to sink with Shumiatsky. Later that year Boris Mokrousov wrote an opera to a libretto by Iosif Prut and V. Dobrozhinsky. Though they introduced several new characters into the plot, Mokrousov told the newspaper *Vecherniaia Moskva* that the central element in the work remained the relationship between Chapaev and Furmanov.[71]

In 1939, in a speech delivered at celebrations of the twentieth anniversary of Soviet cinema, even Dziga Vertov, once the most uncompromising adversary of feature films, was prepared to concede that *Chapaev* had put acted films 'back on the right path' and that acted and documentary films could co-exist.[72] In another celebration of the anniversary, a film compendium, edited by Esfir Shub and Vsevolod Pudovkin *The Cinema Over 20 Years* [Kino za 20 let], released on 27 February 1940, it was natural that an extract from *Chapaev* should be included, along with such masterworks of the silent period as *The Battleship Potemkin, Mother* and *Earth*. At the decade's end, Eisenstein returned to his analysis of the reasons for *Chapaev*'s success, this time considering how the film aroused such strong emotion [*pafos*] in millions of viewers. Noting that overall the film provoked emotion in the opposite way from the 'Odessa Steps' sequence in his own *Battleship Potemkin*, he suggested that the most characteristic episode in *Chapaev* is the '*least* dramatic' one, the illustration of the question 'Where should the Commander be?'

> For this is precisely the episode that introduced into our Soviet film practice something principally, stylistically and qualitatively new. For one of the most emotional features of *Chapaev* was the fact that here *the hero was not placed on a pedestal.*

Just as Chapaev insisted that the commander should not always be in front of his men, but should sometimes remain behind them, so the Vasilev Brothers understood that emotion should not always 'rush forward with sabre unsheathed'. He continued:

> It really is the case that in Chapaev, what it is customary to speak of in the form of a hymn, in elevated speech, in verse, was said in simple colloquial speech.

Only in three episodes, the Kappelite attack, the scene in which Chapaev is shot and wounded in the garret and the explosion at the end of the film, do the Brothers revert to the direct evocation of strong emotion. What unites *Potemkin* and *Chapaev*, Eisenstein concludes, is their shared capacity to arouse strong emotion, but they differ in the way in which they do so.[73]

Chapaev as cinematic model

Dziga Vertov had suggested that *Chapaev* had put Soviet feature films back on the right path, and its influence is clear in other films set in the Civil War. The children's film *Fedka*, made at Lenfilm in 1936 and directed by Nikolai Lebedev, was released on Soviet Army Day, 23 February 1937. Set in 1919, it tells the story of a young boy whose father has been executed by the Whites. Fedka joins up with a brigade of Red Cavalry and becomes the driver of a carriage, harnessed with a troika of horses and carrying a machine gun. Scene after scene is visually reminiscent of the Vasilev Brothers' film and *Fedka* became known as 'the children's *Chapaev*'.

But the most striking manifestation of the desire to follow the *Chapaev* model is in the commissioning of a spate of films about other Civil War commanders. At the first meeting of the Presidium of the Central Executive Committee of the Party since the Seventh Congress of Soviets, held in the Kremlin on 27 February 1935, awards were handed out to film-makers. As Alexander Dovzhenko was being given the Order of Lenin, Stalin called out: 'He has an obligation – a

'Ukrainian *Chapaev*', a fact reported on the front page of *Pravda* the following day.[74] A little later at the same meeting he asked Dovzhenko if he knew of Shchors and added 'think about him'. On 5 March *Pravda* carried both of Stalin's remarks in a lengthy article about the life of Mykola (Nikolai) Shchors, a Ukrainian Red Army commander who was killed fighting against the Poles on 30 August 1919, only a few days before Chapaev.[75] The subject came up again at discussion with Shumiatsky after a Kremlin film screening on 13 March, though on this occasion Stalin insisted that the newspapers were wrong to suggest that he had had only Shchors in mind since 'there were others.'[76] Nevertheless, on 22 May and again on 10 November, Dovzhenko was summoned to the Kremlin to hear Stalin's ideas about the film on Shchors. On the latter occasion, Stalin made Dovzhenko sit down and watch *Chapaev* with him and talked right through the screening, stressing which parts worked the best.[77] Several other meetings with Stalin and other Party officials followed over the tortuous four years of the film's making. The lead actor was changed twice. Eventually the film premiered on 2-3 April 1939 in Moscow and on 1 May 1939 in Kiev. Officially, of course, Dovzhenko was fulsome in his praise of Stalin's 'help' on the film. Awestruck that 'in the midst of work on matters of enormous state importance Comrade Stalin found the time to remember an artist', he recalled Stalin's detailed description, during the 22 May 1935 meeting, of what he would expect a film about Shchors to contain.[78] Privately he was more frank, writing to a friend on 8 December 1939:

> I completed Shchors. It was a very difficult film to make and took a good five years of health from me. And I have still not got over it.[79]

Evidence that Stalin's ambitions were not confined to the Ukraine is offered by an inadvertently comic letter to him of 13 May 1936 from N.F. Gikalo, the Secretary of the Central Committee of the Belorussian Communist Party and N.M. Gololed, the Chairman of the Soviet of People's Commissars of Belorussia:

Much Respected Comrade Stalin!
> Following your instructions, passed to us through Comrade Gololed, about making a film *The Belorussian Chapaev*, we have already set about gathering the necessary material. But we have hit a difficulty in the basic question – whom to take as the main hero of this film, that is to say whom to take as the *Belorussian Chapaev*. A number of people whom we examined are clearly not suitable for

such a big task which you set us and in which the heroism of the Civil War must be concentrated.

Considering this to be a matter of exceptional importance, and knowing that you are personally aware of a considerable number of real heroes of the Civil War, including on the Western Front, on which you were the organiser of victories, as on other Fronts – we turn to you, Comrade Stalin, with a request that you grant us a meeting about this question and help us by prompting us with (naming) the *Belorussian Chapaev*, as you helped the Ukrainians by saying the name Shchors. [...][80]

Though Stalin did not see the comrades till 2 December, and nothing came directly from their request, other films about Civil War commanders who had given their lives for the Revolution were made in Central Asian evacuation after the Soviet Union entered the Second World War. In 1942 Leonid Lukov made *Alexander Parkhomenko*, the story of a Ukrainian peasant who rose to fight against Petliura, the Germans and the Poles in the Ukraine and along the Don, before being killed by the forces of Nestor Makhno on 3 January 1921. The same year Alexander Faintsimmer directed a film about the Moldavian Grigori Kotovsky, who also fought on the Southern Front against Petliura, the Whites and Romanian Interventionists, and has been described by Evgeni Dobrenko as a 'Bessarabian Robin Hood' (*Kotovsky*, 1942). Though Kotovsky survived the Civil War he was murdered in mysterious circumstances in 1925.[81] The genre was revived for the half century of the Revolution, with Alexander Gordon's *Sergei Lazo* (1967), about a commander, born just outside Kishinev, who fought against the Whites and the Interventionists in the Far East, and was killed by the Japanese in May 1920, while *On the Track of the Wolf* [Po volch´emu sledu], a further version of Kotovsky's life, based on his memoirs, was directed by Valeriu Gazhiu in 1976.

Chapaev's reception abroad

Less than two weeks after the film's release *Pravda* announced that copies were going to be sent to France and the USA.[82] It opened in New York on 12 January 1935, and ran there for thirteen weeks, also moving on to other cities. As Jeremy Hicks has shown, in a fascinating comparison of the American and British reception of the film, *Chapaev* was very well received in America, even being named by the National Board of Review as the best foreign film of the year.[83] It was praised in particular for its capacity to entertain, the *New York Herald Tribune* reviewer perhaps finding the key to its later popularity among American audiences by suggesting that it worked 'on the formula of the hard-riding, hard-fighting wild western melodrama of the American cinema', while the *New York Times* critic noted that the film lacked the usual 'grim and labored' defence of Soviet ideology.[84] The film's American success was reported at length in *Izvestiia* on 20 February 1935, with quotations from a number of American papers. Senwald was quoted as naming *Chapaev* one of the three best films of the season, along with *David Copperfield* (1935, directed by George Cukor) and *The Lives of a Bengal Lancer* (1935, directed by Henry Hathaway), and predicting that it would make the year's Top 10 list. The Soviet report concludes that the success of *Chapaev* goes way beyond that of Soviet film art as such and 'acquires the character of yet another great moral victory of the USSR among broad swathes of Americans'.[85] Ten days later, *Pravda* wrote about the film's success in very similar terms. It reported that the film was now showing in several American cities, and quoted at length from the ecstatic American reviews before announcing '*Chapaev* has conquered! Soviet cinema has conquered!'[86]

Chapaev was first shown in England on 10 February 1935, at the Film Society, a private club dedicated to showing foreign-language films which had shown several masterpieces of the Soviet avant-garde at the end of the 1920s. The Film Society's programme notes had warned viewers that though the film's dialogue was 'more racy and full of character than is usual in Soviet talking films', this would be lost without subtitles. It had attempted to suggest some of the detail of the plot by providing explanatory titles before each sequence, but the reviews next day in both the *Times* and the *Manchester Guardian* were negative. Under the unenticing headline 'Civil War in Turkestan', the *Times* found that the Film Society's warning 'does not exaggerate', since 'the humour was of a simple kind, and the subjects of the conversation of no very great interest to those who are not deep in Russian politics.' For R.H., in the *Manchester Guardian*, the film was 'undeniably monotonous' and it was 'impossible to regard it as entertainment', though he conceded that perhaps the audience could have been more attentive. This view was, however, directly at odds with that of the *Monthly Film Bulletin*, which found that 'the last three reels contain as much action and excitement as any audience could desire', and of the *News Chronicle*, which warmed to the film's humour and thrills. Nevertheless, the film was not released publicly in the UK until three years later, on 6 February 1938, when it ran for six weeks at the Forum Cinema in Villiers Street, London.[87] In his assessment of the huge difference between the American and the British reception of the film, Jeremy Hicks concludes that a major part was played by the effective subtitling of the American print, which led to praise of the film's dialogue, and the clumsiness of the approach to conveying the plot taken by the Film Society. In addition, he speculates that the intellectuals of the Film Society were not an ideal audience for a Soviet talkie, committed as they were to the aesthetic of Soviet avant-garde cinema, and notes that the distribution system for Soviet films was far more effective in the USA.[88]

Despite *Pravda's* early confidence, it was over a year before the film was shown in France. It opened at the Panthéon cinema in Paris on 10 December 1935, and even before that fell victim to émigré polemic, being savagely criticised in a Russian-language paper by the émigré writer Georgi Adamovich, who insisted that he could not understand what its reputation was based on, since it was 'cloying, pale and listless'. Perhaps, he concluded, 'foreigners do not sense its specifically Russian falsity'. He praised the acting of Illarion Pevtsov as Colonel Borozdin, while wondering why he had 'the dull eyes of a drug addict and libertine'. He was impressed by the episodes of battle, especially the cavalry charge by Chapaev's division, but overall he found the film 'boring and wearisome'.[89]

This was not, of course, an assessment of the film that could be conveyed to Soviet readers, and a survey of its French reception in *Pravda* on 15 December 1935 quoted the opposing view of *Le Peuple* that the film was well acted and constantly interesting.[90] In May 1936 *Izvestiia* reported that the French firm Nord-Film was translating the Russian text of the film since the directors of more than 300 French cinemas had expressed a desire to show it.[91] Writing in *Iskusstvo kino* the following year, the leading French film critic Georges Sadoul described *Chapaev* as 'first class' and contrasted it favourably with recent American productions.[92] *Chapaev* was apparently banned, however, in French Algeria, where it could be seen as inflammatory. It was eventually shown in independent Algeria in 1964, and praised as reflecting 'truth to life in its revolutionary development'.[93]

The scenes involving the Czechoslovak Corps provoked lively press polemics in Czechoslovakia, where the film was released in 1935, though it was banned for young people and in Slovakia.[94] But perhaps the most remarkable foreign reception was in Republican Spain. The Second Battalion of the Thirteenth International Brigade, formed in December 1936, was named after Chapaev and initially composed predominantly of men from the Balkans. One of the commanders of the Fifteenth Brigade, the Hungarian Mihályi Szalvai, gave himself the pseudonym 'Major Chapaev', while Jock Cunningham, a British commander who had earlier spent two years in prison for leading a mutiny of the Argyle and Sutherland Highlanders in Jamaica, went under the name of the 'English Chapaev'.[95]

Chapaev was widely shown to Republican audiences and seen by the writers Ilia Erenburg and Mikhail Koltsov, who both arrived in Spain in August 1936 to report on the war, Erenburg for *Izvestiia* and Koltsov for *Pravda*. Erenburg arranged for money to be sent from Moscow to purchase a van and a film projector and copies were sent from Moscow of *Chapaev* and Efim Dzigan's *We are From Kronstadt* [My iz Kronshtadta, 1936]. In December 1936, he showed *Chapaev* to Republican troops in a requisitioned church near Teruel. According to the report which he sent to *Izvestiia*, the killing of the sentries by the Whites provoked his audience to pass a resolution to increase their own watchfulness and at the end of the film he was asked 'Señor, please thank Commander Chapaev for his noble example.'[96]

Mikhail Koltsov saw the film in the small Aragonese town of Tardienta on 13 August 1936. The audience were wrapt, since both the landscape and the plot of the film reminded them of their own struggle. When Petka told Chapaev that he was 'Napoleon. A real Napoleon!', the audience recalled that Napoleon had been in these parts 128 years earlier. When they saw Chapaev drown in the Ural River it reminded them of the Ebro, and provoked a cry 'Onward to Zaragoza!'[97] There was an equally enthusiastic reaction when he saw the film again in a crowded Madrid cinema on 7 November 1936, the nineteenth anniversary of the Russian Revolution. When Chapaev told Petka that 'Chapai has never retreated', 'three thousand people shouted in reply: "Viva Russia, Viva!"'[98] A young Englishman, Bernard Knox, later to be Professor of Classics at Yale, was serving on the northwest sector of the Madrid Front in the French Battalion of the XIth International Brigade. He too saw the film in Madrid, in December, and was particularly struck by the Maxim gun.

> They were exactly the guns we were now using (we had exchanged our Lewis guns for them some time in November), but in the film, the partisans had them pulled by teams of horses, while we had dragged them over the bumps and pits in the Casa de Campo and up and down the staircases of Filosofia y Letras with our bare and half-frozen hands.[99]

In a five month period in 1938, 418,000 people in Republican Spain saw the film.[100] Speaking of the effect of the film years later, Dolores Ibárruri, 'La Pasionaria', recalled:

The scene of the "psychic" attack made a particular impression. [...] This scene had a particular significance for the fighters. The explanation is very simple. Our fighters were fighting against the regular army. They were not soldiers themselves,they were members of the voluntary militia and they were worse armed than their enemy, and naturally it was very hard for our people to resist the enemy's frontal attack. And when the Kappelites appeared on screen, advancing in their frontal 'psychic attack', and Chapaev's troops respond steadfastly with machine-gun fire, after first letting them get up close, this was very uplifting for the Spanish fighters, and aroused a desire to do likewise.[101]

Chapaev during The Second World War

Germany invaded Russia on 22 June 1941. It was a Sunday, and Ivan Bolshakov, who had been in charge of the State Committee for Cinematographic Affairs since June 1939, was telephoned at his dacha and summoned to the Kremlin, where he was told to remove all the films that were showing on Moscow screens and replace them with historical ones, '*Alexander Nevsky, Minin and Pozharsky, Suvorov, Chapaev, Shchors*, and also all the anti-Fascist films'. Bolshakov recalls that this was achieved in two hours.[102] On 30 October, his deputy, Nikolai Savchenko, drew up a list of 'films recommended for exhibition during wartime'. Chapaev was one of 24 feature films described as 'particularly recommended'.[103] The film was shown to troops at the Front and partisans performed 'screenings from memory'.[104] Rostislav Iurenev, later to become a prominent scholar of Soviet film, recalls the fighting outside Novorossiisk in autumn 1942. One evening a travelling cinema arrived at the garrison with *Chapaev*. The projectionist complained that the copy was 'completely worn out. Wherever things are hard they send me in with this *Chapaev*'. The film was shown in a destroyed stable, and though the picture kept breaking it worked its magic and going on the attack next morning Iurenev felt as if Chapaev had joined them in their advance.[105] The same idea was widely taken up in wartime propaganda. A famous 1941 poster by the Kukryniksy showed Soviet troops with tanks and fixed bayonets advancing under the shades of Suvorov and of Chapaev and his machine-gun, with the caption 'We fight robustly, we stab desperately, grandsons of Suvorov, children of Chapaev.'[106]

Russia's entry into the war also led, almost inadvertently at first, to renewed interest in the film in Britain. The 19 July 1941 issue of *Picture Post* carried an extensive feature on 'The Russian Soldier', headed by a large illustration with the caption 'The Russian soldier as the Russian

people see him'. The picture is the famous shot from the film of
Chapaev and Petka firing their Maxim gun.[107] The following year the
film was re-released in Britain, and attracted a favourable review in the
Sunday Times from Dilys Powell, who felt that '*Chapaev* helps us to
understand Russia better than any other film.'[108]

Chapaev himself also became a 'participant' in the Great Patriotic
War. The fact that the Vasilev Brothers' film contained no shots of his
dead body made it possible for wartime tellers of tales to 'resurrect' him
to fight in the Battle of Stalingrad and to join the Russian army's march
on Berlin.[109] He was also brought back to life in the short film *Chapaev is
With Us* [Chapaev s nami] directed by Vladimir Petrov in the first days
of the war and released on 31 July. It begins with the ending of the
Vasilev Brothers' film, but this time, instead of drowning in the river,
Chapaev gets to the other side, fulfilling the dream of countless Soviet
schoolboys. A Soviet soldier and airman are waiting with his white
horse. As he emerges they say: 'At last, Vasili Ivanych. We've been
waiting for you. We thought you wouldn't make it!', to which he retorts,
'What! Chapaev wouldn't make it?!' Dressed now in his fur hat and felt
cloak he asks: 'What's going on here? Have the Germans got through
again?' Told that this is indeed the case he summons the men to horse
and makes a stirring speech, recalling his own heroic exploits and the
promises he made. To documentary footage of marching Soviet troops
he reminds them that they have magnificent weaponry and magnificent
troops, and that the entire people is with them, 'a people the like of
which there is probably no other in the whole of Europe.' He binds them
with a Chapaevan oath of loyalty and tells them that he, too, is always
with them. To the music of Tchaikovsky Soviet tanks, planes and
paratroopers advance on the enemy. Babochkin recalls that when they
were shooting it outside Leningrad there were German planes
overhead.[110] A similar approach is taken in *The Song of Chapaev* [Pesnia
o Chapaeve, 1944], directed by Olga Khodataeva and Petr Nosov. A
mixture of live action and animation, the film opens in mid-winter with
World War Two Red Cavalrymen warming themselves before a bonfire
in a wood. As one of the fighters sings the title song, Chapaev's men
appear in animation, and at their head on a white horse, his cloak flying
in the wind, his sabre raised, Vasili Ivanych himself. This is followed by
scenes of Whites sacking a village and Chapaev riding to the rescue. As
he fells his enemy, the action cuts back to the present, to this 'Chapaev
brigade', inspired by his heroic example. The film end with the words
'people will not forget'.

Chapaev's influence is also apparent in the plots of new films set in
the Second World War. In *No Greater Love*, for example, the heroine

Praskovia, who has become the leader of a group of partisans, mercilessly shoots a deserter who wants to stop fighting and go back home. She becomes a surrogate mother for a young couple, Senia and Fenia, and even presides over their forest marriage, but they emulate the experience of Petka and Anna when Senia dies heroically. As befits a film made during wartime, however, Praskovia does not die like Chapaev, surviving to make a stirring patriotic speech at the film's end.

The Post-War Years
In the context of the heightened ideological control which was re-imposed in the Soviet Union after the end of the War, it is not perhaps surprising to find the director Grigori Roshal suggesting in 1948: 'In truth, *Chapaev* is not just a film about Chapaev. It is a film about Lenin and Stalin, although Lenin and Stalin do not appear in it.'[111] There is a far more incisive interpretation of the film in the brilliant dissection of the cinematic Stalin cult written two years later by André Bazin. In terms of their characters' humanity, says Bazin, 'the masterpiece of Soviet films with historic heroes is surely *Chapaev*', and he notes 'with what intelligence the failings of Chapaev, even in his manifestly most historic acts, are suggested without diminishing him at all psychologically'. He finds in the film both a glorification of Chapaev and a warning that a long-term political strategy is more useful than the 'deeds of the heroic and temporarily useful leader of a gang'. Later in the study Bazin explicitly contrasts Chapaev with the cinematic Stalin, who cannot be defined through character, psychology or personality.[112]

The late Soviet reception
The same combination of bland official approval, serious critical attention and broad general popularity that had characterised the film's early reception is still apparent during the Thaw years. In 1956 *Chapaev* earned a long essay by Nikolai Lebedev in the third volume of a new history of Soviet cinema, an essay which ends conventionally by describing the film as 'an outstanding work of cinematic Socialist Realism' and 'a model to be copied, an example on which the Party orientated the masters of Soviet cinema'.[113] In another weighty official volume, issued the following year to survey the achievements of Soviet cinema for the fortieth anniversary of the Revolution, Nikolai Pogodin called it 'one of those works which never die'.[114] But in a lecture to student directors at Mosfilm Studios the same year, the director Mikhail Romm said:

But let's speak honestly, what is magnificent about *Chapaev*? In *Chapaev* there is a magnificent script and one magnificent actor. Khersonsky was partly right: the film is badly shot by the cinematographer [...] the other actors are not up to much. A whole series of episodes are remarkable for their far from brilliant taste, like, for example 'Mitka is dying, he wants some fish soup', – suddenly out of a completely different film there appears this strange Mitka, asking for fish soup.

[...] There are no irreproachable and sacred pictures, and *Chapaev* is not irreproachable, and when you look at the film you can and should discover an enormous number of professional shortcomings in it. [...]
Eisenstein also fell into rapture about Chapaev, but I'm convinced that in private he 'made mincemeat' of the Vasilevs.[115]

Despite Romm's strictures, *Chapaev's* continuing popularity in the late Soviet years was also reflected in the frequency with which it was alluded to in new films, through emulation of its plot, through re-imagining its hero or through direct reference to the cult the film had inspired. Alas, constraints of space make it possible to mention only some of these films here. Iurii Egorov's *They Were First* [Oni byli pervymi, 1956], set in 1918, tells the story of the first generation of Young Communists and their participation in the fight for Soviet power. The Chapaev model is clearly apparent in episodes which combine heroic fighting with doomed and sacrificed love. In Ivan Lukinsky's hugely popular story about a demobbed soldier, *Ivan Brovkin in the Virgin Lands* [Ivan Brovkin na tseline, 1958], Ivan is ill in hospital when he is asked to become a brigadier, a leader of a work group. Attempting to explain how he thinks the tractors should be deployed he grabs objects from his bedside table and lays them out across the floor, just as Chapaev had done with his potatoes, earning himself the sobriquet Chapai. In the same year Chapaev again became the hero of an animated film in Mikhail Tsekhanovsky's *The Tale of Chapaev* [Skaz o Chapaeve], in which the waves of the Ural River carry him safely to the other bank and nature helps him to continue to fight the Whites, and the drawn Chapaev has both the features and the voice of Boris Babochkin.

A perhaps surprising fan of the film was Andrey Tarkovsky. When the lonely boy and the adult working man plan a visit to the cinema in his diploma film *The Steamroller and the Violin* [Katok i skripka, 1960], it is of course *Chapaev* that they intend to see. Tarkovsky explained his enthusiasm for the film in February 1967, when he discussed the treatment of character in Soviet historical films in connection with his own Andrei Rublev:

> Just think, a man who doesn't know what the International is, who gets into conflict with his commissar, who announces that the commander should be not in   front on his fighting steed but behind his brigade, a man who perishes, who fights in his underwear – you would think that everything here is the reverse of the ideal cinematic character. And it is only thanks to the fact that we see in him an ordinary, normal man that he becomes immortal in our eyes. Chapaev as played by Babochkin is a unique phenomenon. And of course honour and praise to the Vasilev Brothers who edited a film of ordinary length out of enough material for an enormous epic film, but what a film, it's all like a diamond, with every facet contrasting with another, which is what character develops from. What grandeur! This is what a real historical film is! [...] Because the hero is a human being, and that is why he is immortal.[116]

In 1964, the thirtieth anniversary of the film's release was marked by its re-release with a restored soundtrack, an event widely marked in the press.[117] Two years later a book about the film appeared in the prestigious *Masterworks of Soviet Cinema* series. It combined the script of the film, illustrated by hundreds of frame stills, with examples of the film's reception at home and abroad over fifty years and memoirs of the filming by the Vasilev Brothers and Boris Babochkin.

1967, the year of the fiftieth anniversary of the Russian Revolution, naturally witnessed a sustained attention to the events of the Revolution and the Civil War, which in cinematic terms was expressed both by the revival of classic films and by the commissioning of new treatments of Revolutionary themes. Watching *Chapaev* on Soviet television at the beginning of the year, the writer Fedor Abramov was shocked by his own reaction. On 8 January 1967 he wrote in his diary:

> *Chapaev*. How I used to love that film! But I've just watched it on TV and I was horrified (the psychic attack).
> Because it's self-extermination. The murder of the best, the brightest people on both sides [...]
> And for the first time that evening my romantic feelings became unsteady (withered). And everything fell into place.
> The Civil War as the madness of a nation. This is not the way to

resolve national problems. And it is no coincidence that civil wars have become things of the past. The only nations which have recourse to them now are undeveloped ones.[118]

Chapaev's influence is apparent in several of the new films on Civil War themes, including Evgenii Karelov's *There Were Two Comrades In The Army* [Sluzhili dva tovarishcha, 1968] and Miklós Jancsó's Russian-Hungarian co-production *The Red and the White* [Csillagosok, katonák, 1967], set, like *Chapaev*, in the Volga region in 1919. The theme is treated more lightly in Vladimir Motyl's hugely successful *The White Sun of the Desert* [Beloe solntse pustyni, 1969], set in Central Asia after the Civil War, which tells the story of the demobbed Red Army soldier Fedor Sukhov, his sidekick Petrukha, and Petrukha's doomed love for the beautiful Giulchatai. The phenomenon continues in films about military men through the 1970s and 1980s.

Chapaev also remained a hero of adventure films for children. In *Chapaev's Little Eagles* [Orliata Chapaeva, 1968], directed by Iuri Pobedonostsev, the boy hero becomes a clerk in Chapaev's division, and actually meets Chapaev himself. The same story gets a dream variant in Radomir Vasilevsky's *A Step off the Roof* [Shag s kryshi, 1970], in which a modern-day schoolboy, dreaming of becoming a hero, is transported to various historical epochs, but finds true heroism only among the men of Chapaev's division. In *Where are you, Chapai?* [Gde ty, Chapai?, 1984], directed by Talgat Temenov, the setting is a Kazakh village when the boys are playing a game of Reds and Whites. The game gets out of hand and 'Petka the orderly' gets beaten up by the Whites, but he bravely wipes away his tears and reports back to his Commander.

The frequency with which the films of the Brezhnev years referred to Chapaev is but one sign of the pervasiveness of the Chapaev cult in late Soviet Russia. By this time Chapaev had given his name to villages and towns, to streets, squares, and a river steamer, and was commemorated in innumerable statues. He had appeared in paintings, on postcards, and on the lids of the famous Palekh lacquered boxes. But perhaps the greatest measure of his now mythical status came in the popular anecdotes which grew up about him, Petka and Anna in the 1960s and 1970s. According to Andrei Krasniashchikh, two factors are necessary for a cinematic character to become the hero of anecdotes: audiences must have become bored with him through the endless showing of the film on television, and the character himself must have something inhuman about him – even the original cinematic Chapaev was a kind of monument to himself.[119] But in the view of Alexander Genis, this only increases the character's status, since 'images become great only when they leave the culture which gave birth to them in order to dissolve in the element of folklore.'[120] Superficially simple, these anecdotes are in fact highly sophisticated engagements with the mythology of Soviet life. If they contain a strong element of mockery, usually representing Chapaev as none too bright, it is not so much the character himself who is being mocked as the cult which has grown up around him and the general absurdity of official Soviet life. Chapaev himself is always viewed with wry affection, in part because his qualities in the anecdotes mirror those which ordinary Russians like to ascribe to themselves.[121] In the words of the writer Viktor Pelevin:

> Everyone who lived in Soviet Russia is indebted to Chapaev for minutes of laughter and happiness, for which there were relatively few causes in real life. The folkloric part of the Chapaev myth was like a prayer of the entire people, as a result of which somewhere in the world of forms the image coalesced of another Chapaev, considerably more real than his pale historical double.[122]

Some anecdotes re-work episodes of the film, while others transport Chapaev, Petka and Anka into contemporary life. Repeatedly Chapaev misunderstands both complicated words and simple information. In one of them Anka has just moved into a new flat and invites Chapaev and Petka to a house-warming party. 'Take bus No. 93', she tells Chapaev. But Vasili Ivanovich never turns up. Next morning Petka runs into him standing at the bus-stop. 'Good thing you got here', says Chapaev. 'I've been counting them. That was bus No. 92. The next one we can take to Anka's'.[123] In another, Chapaev comes to see Anka and finds that she has no clothes on. 'Why are you naked?' he asks. 'It's because I haven't got any dresses', she replies. So Vasili Ivanych opens her wardrobe. 'What do you mean?' he says, 'one dress, two dresses, oh, hallo, Petka. Three dresses, four dresses...' Seth Graham has described the qualities of the Chapaev of popular anecdote in the following terms:

> There is a leitmotif in the anekdot-al Chapaev's constant misapprehension of language, and indeed in his behaviour in general. He perceives the world through a filter of carnality, rather than ideology or military values. His motivations are food, sleep, drink, tobacco, sex, gambling and the chance to use profanity.[124]

In the official hypostasis, Chapaev is a 'folk archetype corrupted in the service of a value system alien to folk traditions. Anekdoty are hyperbolic correctives to that bogus use of his image.'[125] Thus this affectionate elevation of the base elements in Chapaev's (and the Russian) character is yet another sign of his mythical immortality.

At the same time as his rebirth in the popular imagination, Chapaev was still the recipient of regular formal celebration. In 1974, for the fortieth anniversary of the film's appearance, a second opera was commissioned, this time from Alexander Kholminov, while the fiftieth anniversary, in 1984, was also widely celebrated. The words of the great director Marlen Khutsiev are typical. He recalled the film as the first love of his childhood, a 'textbook of inspiration':

> There is no limit to my love of that film. I use the word 'film' and I experience an involuntary feeling of embarrassment at using such an ordinary, everyday word to describe such an enormous, staggering, stunning phenomenon as *Chapaev*.[126]

Chapaev in the new Russia
At the end of the 1980s and in the 1990s Russian culture combined a now overt irony towards the symbols of the Soviet world with serious attempts to understand the past and its links with the Soviet and post-Soviet present. In this context *Chapaev* could be at one and the same time the object of mockery, of unthinking appropriation and of thoughtful and original critical analysis. At one end of the scale, the avant-garde film group *Kinogruppa Chepaev*, led by the film scholar Sergei Dobrotvorsky, which emerged in 1986, found its title by combining the name of Vasili Ivanych with that of one of the most popular 'rebel heroes' of recent decades, Che Guevara. The contradictions of late Soviet popular culture are wonderfully captured in one of their cartoons, in which Chapaev and Che meet Mao Tse Tung while examining a new model of the Maxim gun.[127] Another avant-garde group, *Krasnyi matros*, produced a charmingly ironic illustrated edition of F.P. Buzaev's 1938 tale 'Chapai', complete with his magic sabre and rifle, in 2000.[128]

There is a similar affectionately sardonic quality to some of the cinematic quotations of the film in these years. In Juliusz Machulski's Soviet-Polish gangster film parody *Déjà vu* [Dezha viu, 1988] it is a gangster who emulates Chapaev by firing a machine-gun from a circular oriel window, and there is further ornamental use of the film in Rashid Nugmanov's post-Communist pastiche Western *Wild East* [Dikii vostok, 1993]. The leader of a gang of dwarfs follows Chapaev in giving a lesson in tactics by moving potatoes around a table. When this bemuses one of them he asks him 'don't you go to the cinema?'[129] Not that this ludic impulse was to everyone's taste. Speaking at the fourth Congress of the Union of Film-Makers of the Russian Federation in May 1988, soon after he had taken over its chairmanship, the director Nikita Mikhalkov lamented the current state of Russian cinema in the following terms:

> Who is going to be a hero for our children? Who are they going to tell anecdotes about as we did about Vasili Ivanovich Chapaev and Stirlits? Without this folklore there can be no cinema. Man cannot live without a hero. He must have an image, he must have a symbol. [...] But see how all the children know who Stallone is, all the children know who Schwarzenegger is, because it is through their heroes that American cinema teaches its children the concepts of honour, and justice.[130]

Chapaev is at the heart of one the most profound and radical examinations of post-Soviet society, Petr Lutsik's *Outskirts* [Okraina, 1998], released within months of Mikhalkov making his remarks, but Lutsik's use of the popular hero is anything but conventional. Though the title of the film refers back to another classic of 1930s Soviet cinema, Boris Barnet's 1933 film *Outskirts*, it is largely through allusion to *Chapaev* that Lutsik offers his grim analysis of post-Soviet society. Set in the 1990s, the film tells the story of a rebellion by a group of Urals peasants who have been deprived of their land by the new co-operative farmers. At their head is the former collective farm chairman and World War Two hero, Vasili Ivanovich Perfilev. They decide to go to Moscow, to seek out their real enemy, an oligarch who wants to take control of their land and drill it for oil. The film is pervaded by Gavriil Popov's music for *Chapaev* and before embarking upon their search for justice they sing 'The Death of Ermak'. Vasili Ivanych is killed along the way, but the others proceed to Moscow where they avenge him by destroying the oligarch's high rise building by fire. Everything about *Outskirts*, from the Urals setting, to the music, to the plot, to 'Vasili Ivanych', to the actors' physiognomies, relates back to *Chapaev*, but all of these elements of the film are used to tell a tale of the defiant rejection of authority, rather than a realisation of its rightness. This Vasili Ivanych is possessed by loathing for the Communist Party and its representative because of their craven collusion with the new men of power, and it is Vasili Ivanych's doomed, anarchic peasant cunning that the film celebrates.

The end of Soviet power also ushered in a new debate about the qualities of the film itself. Attending a screening of films about the

Civil War in 1990, and hearing the audience's applause when Chapaev's troops appeared, the writer Tatiana Tolstaia was assailed by exactly the same thoughts which Fedor Abramov had confided to his diary in 1967. When the lights went on she got up on stage:

> This applause is servile. And not understanding that is catastrophic. The feelings which gave rise to it have ruined our country and continue to ruin what is left of it. It is the notorious 'class feeling' which is at work. We have seen part of our people go against another part, brother move against his own brother. What are you applauding?[131]

Chapaev snacks and Chapaev computer games

A new anxiety about the film's reputation and reception was also apparent in the studio discussion after it was screened in 1994, the year of the film's sixtieth anniversary, in the pioneering television series *Kinopravda? (Film Truth?)*.[132] These screenings were devoted to the reassessment of key ideologically charged works of the Soviet cinematic past, and on this occasion attitudes ranged from enthusiastic support of the film to its complete rejection as a talented but 'clear falsehood' and a justification of an inhuman regime.

Chapaev was also re-born in the post-Soviet years as the hero of a number of works of imaginative prose which attempted to deconstruct

Soviet mythology. In Andrei Levkin's 1993 story 'Chapaev: Birthplace – Riga (New findings about Georgi Gurdzhiev)', Vasili Ivanych is created as a conformist bio-robot, programmed for war, but his anarchic streak comes to the fore, forcing his creators to turn off his energy supply, which brings about his instantaneous demise.[133] In Vasili Aksenov's 'The Ship of Peace the Vasili Chapaev' (1995), a group of Australian members of the International Society for Krishna Consciousness (Hare Krishnas) are plunged into horror on a visit to Samara when they see a statue of Chapaev and 'recognise' in him the embodiment of the Hindu demons Vritri, Madhu and Mur. It is only through the recitation of 1,001 tales from the life of the non-demonic Chapaev of popular anecdote ('Chapaev and Petka are visiting Paris...'), that their Russian guide dissuades them from committing ritual suicide.[134] And in one of the most famous texts of a decade of post-modernist experiment with Soviet myth, Viktor Pelevin blends the heroes of the novel and the film with their subsequent behaviour in Soviet anecdotes, and then adds his own new qualities to the mix. In his 1996 *The Clay Machine-Gun* Chapaev is a Buddhist teacher, Anka a glamorous femme fatale, and Petka is Chapaev's disciple, a Symbolist poet in 1919 who thinks he is a patient in a 1990s Moscow psychiatric hospital – or is it the reverse?[135]

By the century's end, Chapaev, Petka and Anka were the heroes of computer games, of *Petka and Vasili Ivanych save the Galaxy*, of *Petka and Vasili Ivanych 2. Judgement Day*, of *Petka 3. The Return of Alaska*. They also appeared, as eloquent evidence of the new market value of all things Soviet, on the packaging of salted pistachios and of packets of bacon croutons. The Russian name given to this delicacy was *Chapsy*, a play upon the equally popular *chipsy* (crisps), and Vasili Ivanych approached on his foaming steed, in his hand... a tankard of foaming beer.

A hero for the Twenty First Century
At the time the 1990s may have seemed to witness the destruction of the dialogic nature of the Chapaev myth, with the increasingly stolid hero of official propaganda definitively vanquished by the double whose habitat was popular anecdote, advertising and the imagination of a subversive younger generation of writers. Recent years have, however, provided ample evidence of the continuing viability of both sides of the Chapaev cult.

The new century opened with the return of a new cinematic idol, Danila Bagrov, first seen (and immediately loved by audiences) in 1997 in Alexei Balabanov's *Brother* [Brat]. No one could be further from Chapaev, it would seem, than this callow, introverted youth with the

Chapai café bar with 'revolutionary cuisine', Crimea,
Summer 2007

desire to conquer the Moscow criminal underworld. But when, in
Balabanov's sequel, *Brother 2* [Brat 2, 2000], Danila and his brother set
out to avenge the death of a friend, they steal a 'Chapaevan' Maxim
gun from the former Lenin Museum and turn it on the gang who are
pursuing them in a quiet Moscow courtyard. One critic was even

moved to interpret the entire plot and structure of *Brother 2* through the prism of *Chapaev*, suggesting that a new Russian Civil War was being played out in the Moscow scenes of the film, and that in the later American sequences Danila outdid his illustrious forefather, whom lack of knowledge of languages had famously prevented from commanding his army on a world scale.[136]

Songs and re-worked scenes from the film are still widespread in recent Russian cinema. 'The Black Raven' is performed three times by the carousing heroes of Aleksandr Rogozhkin's *Particularities of the National Hunt in the Winter Period* [Osobennosti natsional'noi okhoty v zimnii period, 2000]. In Nikolai Dostal's television series *Punishment Battalion* [Shtrafbat, 2004], which tells a story hitherto ignored in official culture of the men who were taken out of Soviet prison camps to fight at the Front in the Second World War, it is 'The Death of Ermak' which the men sing, led by a priest, before going into their final, mortal encounter with the enemy. There is a particularly ideologically revealing use of an episode from the film in Vitali Vorobev's *Resistance* [Protivostoianie, 2005], also set in the Second World War, in which a Russian reconnaissance scout comes across his brother, who, after a period in German captivity, has gone over to the anti-Soviet forces of General Vlasov. Not having the heart to kill him, he lets him go. Later the brother comes over to the Soviets and gives them news of where the Vlasovite forces are massing. But this seeming change of ideological heart is in fact a trap, which the Soviet forces fall into. The Second World War anti-Soviet Russian forces of General Vlasov are more sinister than the White forces of General Borozdin, who was too upright to consider such a ploy. Nevertheless, in the ensuing encounter the traitor brother is shot, the Vlasovites are exterminated, and somehow most of the reconnaissance group survive.

At the other end of the scale, Chapaev, Anka and his cavalry troops all figure in Iuli Gusman's recent film *Soviet Park* [Park sovetskogo perioda, 2006] (the Russian title explicitly echoes *Park iurskogo perioda*, the Russian title for *Jurassic Park*), in which Soviet civilisation is lovingly re-created in a thriving theme park. But despite an effective impersonation of Chapaev by the popular actor and director Sergei Nikonenko, *Soviet Park* is a toothless, pointless affair, suggesting that it is perhaps the unofficial rather than the official Chapaev who is temporarily, unable to stimulate the artistic imagination.[137]

An interest in uncovering more of the historical truth lies behind the large number of newspaper articles and documentary films about Chapaev and the film which have appeared in recent years. Easily the most controversial of the documentaries was *Chapai's Love* [Liubov'

Chapaia, 2003], directed by Stanislav Razdorsky and Elena Razdorskaia. Using the diaries, letters and memoirs of the protagonists, it follows the course of Chapaev's various love affairs, in particular the love rivalry of Chapaev and Furmanov over Furmanov's wife Anna (Naia) Steshenko. Though the details of this story had been known to literary scholars since the publication of extensive extracts from Furmanov's diary by Pavel Kupriianovsky in 1996, the broad dissemination of the information in a televised documentary provoked consternation and angry protest.[138] And interest in the story remains vivid to this day. In 2007, Russian television aired Tatiana Vardanian's documentary *The True Story of Anka-The Machine-Gunner* [Podlinnaia istoriia Anki-pulemetchitsy], a biography of Mariia Andreevna Popova, whose life had encompassed fighting in the Civil War, a murky period in the Soviet trade delegation in Berlin and years in the camps, and who is considered another prototype of the Vasilev Brothers' Anna.[139]

So *Chapaev* lives on, still generating enthusiasm, curiosity and controversy in varying measure, almost 90 years after his death in the Ural River, more than 80 since the publication of Furmanov's novel, over 70 years after the appearance of the legendary film. September 2007 saw the release of Vitali Melnikov's engaging film *The 'Beat the Enemy' Agit-Brigade* [Agitbrigada 'Bei vraga!', 2007], based upon an episode in his recently published memoirs.[140] It tells the story of a group of young people travelling around the Soviet Far East during the Second World War with the aim of keeping up morale in the struggle against Hitler. They perform sketches, sing to accordion and show films. And of course they show *Chapaev*, even being prepared to wind the end of the film backwards when Chapaev's death in the Ural River causes too much distress, thus following the example of the 1941 propaganda film *Chapaev is with us*. In the affection in which he continues to be held in the Russian popular imagination, Vasili Ivanych has, indeed, swum to the other side.

Notes

Chapter 1

1   This sketch of Chapaev's life is based upon material taken from I.O. Surmina, 'Vasilii Ivanovich Chapaev', in her *Samye znamenitye geroi Rossii*, Moscow, 2002, pp. 336-46; and from E. Chapaeva, *Moi neizvestnyi Chapaev*, Moscow, 2005.

2   For the anecdote see, for example, Chapaeva, *Moi neizvestnyi Chapaev*, p. 15.

3   Chapaeva, p. 248. For Lindov's letter of recommendation, see pp. 238-9. A recent publication dates Chapaev's enrolment into the Academy to 8 December 1918, and dates the letter to either 24 December 1918 or January 1919. It concludes that Chapaev did not spend more than two or three weeks attending lectures. See A. Ganin, 'Chapai v Akademii', *Rodina*, 2008, 4, pp. 93-97 (the letter is reproduced on p. 97).

4   For the overall context of the battle against Kolchak of which Chapaev's activity was a part, see E. Mawdsley, *The Russian Civil War* [1987], Edinburgh, 2000, pp. 134-55.

5   Information on Furmanov's life is taken from P.V. Kupriianovskii, *Iskaniia. Bor'ba. Tvorchestvo (Put' D.A. Furmanova)*, Yaroslavl, 1967.

6   Kupriianovskii, *Iskaniia*, p. 192.

7   Ibid., p. 134.

8   On Military Commissars see 'Komissar voennyi', in I.N. Rodionov *et al.* (eds), *Voennaia entsiklopediia v vos'mi tomakh*, Moscow, 1994-2004, volume 4, 1999, pp. 123-24.

9   Kupriianovskii, *Iskaniia*, p. 230.

10 Furmanov, *Sobranie sochinenii v chetyrekh tomakh*, Moscow, 1960-1961, 4, p. 166. Furmanov's diaries have not been published in anything like their full extent. The edition being used here is the fullest published version.

11 Ibid., pp. 172-3.

12 Ibid., p. 177.
13 Ibid.
14 Ibid., pp. 178-9.
15 Ibid., p. 188
16 Ibid., p. 197
17 Ibid., p. 198
18 Ibid., pp. 199-201
19 Ibid., p. 210
20 Kupriianovskii, *Iskaniia*, pp. 215-16.
21 Ibid., p. 223.
22 P.V. Kupriianovskii, *Neizvestnyi Furmanov,* Ivanovo, 1996, pp. 132-5.
23 Ibid., pp. 132-3.
24 Ibid., p. 134.
25 Ibid., p. 135.
26 Kupriianovskii, *Iskaniia*, p. 224.
27 Ibid., p. 226.
28 Kupriianovskii, *Neizvestnyi*, pp. 136-7.
29 Ibid., pp. 137-8.
30 See for example the plan published by M. Sotskova in her afterword to the publication of the novel in Furmanov, *Sobranie sochinenii*, 1, pp. 329-30.
31 The 2003 documentary film *Liubov´ Chapaia* (Chapaev's Love) will be discussed in Chapter 4 of this study.
32 Furmanov, *Sobranie sochinenii*, 4, p. 287.
33 Ibid., pp. 289-90.
34 Ibid., p. 291.
35 Subsequent publications are based on this revised fourth edition. The edition used here will be that in D. Furmanov, *Sobranie sochinenii*, volume 1, 'Chapaev', 1960, pp. 23-326.
36 Furmanov, *Sobranie sochinenii*, 1, pp. 50-1.
37 Ibid., p. 63.
38 Ibid., p. 83.
39 For an examination of this dialectic, and its role in Soviet culture, see K. Clark, *The Soviet Novel. History as Ritual*, Chicago, 1981, pp. 15-24.
40 Furmanov, *Sobranie sochinenii*, 1, p.89.
41 Ibid., p. 108.
42 Ibid., pp. 158-9.
43 Elan´ (who is called Sizov in some editions of the novel) is based upon the figure of Ivan Semenovich Kutiakov, Commander of the 1st (73rd) Brigade of Chapaev's 25th Division. After Chapaev's death he became Commander of the Division: Furmanov, *Sobranie sochinenii*, 4, pp. 186-7, 494-5. He contributed an article, 'Chapaev i "Chapaev"',

and a biographical sketch, 'Iz biografii Vasiliia Ivanovicha Chapaeva', to the first book about the film, *Chapaev. O fil'me*, Moscow, 1936, pp. 31-48, 267-306. He fell victim to the purges in May 1937.

44 Furmanov, *Sobranie sochinenii*, 1, p. 308.

45 Ibid., pp. 308-9. Here, as in many passages in the book, the contrast with the Vasil'ev Brothers' film is instructive.

46 Ibid., p. 310.

47 Ibid., p. 326.

48 R. Vroon, 'Dmitrii Furmanov's *Chapaev* and the aesthetics of the Russian Avant-Garde', in J. Bowlt and O. Matich (eds), *Laboratory of Dreams. The Russian Avant-Garde and Cultural Experiment*, Stanford, 1996, pp. 219-34 (p. 233).

49 These rumours were at the base of a story by Boris Pil'niak, 'Povest' nepogashennoi luny' ('The Tale of the Untextinguished Moon'), which appeared in January 1926, but was immediately banned.

50 Furmanov, *Sobranie sochinenii*, 4, p. 320.

51 M. Gor'kii, letter to Furmanov of 27 August 1925, quoted from his *Pis'ma o literature*, ed. A. I. Ovcharenko, Moscow, 1957, p. 307.

52 For a report on this discussion and a survey of the two writers' relationship, see 'Furmanov i Babel'', publ. L. K. Kuvanova, in I. I. Anisimov *et al.* (eds), *Literaturnoe nasledstvo*, volume 74, *Iz tvorcheskogo naslediia sovetskikh pisatelei*, Moscow, 1965, pp. 500-12.

53 Furmanov, *Sobranie sochinenii*, 4, pp. 342-3.

54 On Furmanov as Babel''s editor, see, for example, I. Babel', *Detstvo i drugie rasskazy*, ed. E. Sicher, Jerusalem, 1979, p. 364.

55 On echoes of Red Cavalry in the film *Chapaev*, see Chapter 3 of this study. On Babel''s reaction to the film, see Chapter 4.

56 'Dmitrii Furmanov', in O.D. Golubeva *et al.* (eds), *Russkie sovetskie pisateli. Prozaiki. Biobibliograficheskii ukazatel'*, volume 5, Moscow, 1968, p. 550.

57 Ibid.

58 Clark, *The Soviet Novel*, p. 85. For a rewarding analysis of Furmanov's novel, see Ibid., pp. 84-9.

Chapter 2

1 Diary entry of 26 June 1923, Furmanov, *Sobranie sochinenii*, 4, p. 320.

2 On this see Kupriianovskii, *Iskaniia*, pp. 363-4, and I. Dolinskii, *Chapaev. Dramaturgiia*, Moscow, 1945, pp. 10-11.

3 Furmanov, *Sobranie sochinenii*, 4, p. 335.

4 Babel''s letter to Furmanov of 21 August 1925, quoted from I. Babel', *Sochineniia v 2-kh tomakh*, ed. A. Pirozhkova, Moscow, 1990, volume 1, p. 243. The 'anniversary film "the year 1905"' is Sergei

Eizenshtein's *The Strike*.

5 See G. Roberts, *Forward Soviet! History and Non-Fiction Film in the USSR*, London and New York, 1999, p. 59.

6 Dolinskii, *Chapaev*, pp. 12-18 (p. 16).

7 Dolinskii, *Chapaev*, p. 24.

8 This is the contention of E. Peremyshlev, 'Brat′ia Vasil′evy', http://www.ruthenia.ru/moskva/encycl/b/br_vas.htm

9 Since this film has not survived, it is difficult to be sure how to translate its title, which could also be rendered as *A Private Affair or Personal File*.

10 The sketch of the biography and early career of the Vasil′ev Brothers is taken from D. Pisarevskii, *Brat′ia Vasil′evy*, Moscow, 1981, pp. 21-90, and from 'Kratkaia khronologiia zhizni i tvorchestva G.N. i S.D. Vasil′evykh', in Brat′ia Vasil′evy, *Sobranie sochinenii v 3 tomakh*, Moscow, 1981–1983, volume 3, 1983, pp. 539-54.

11 Pisarevskii, *Brat′ia Vasil′evy*, pp. 37-8. Initially the Brothers thought of casting in the role of Chapaev Nikolai Batalov, already a star actor after playing Pavel Vlasov in Vsevolod Pudovkin's *Mother* [Mat′, 1926], Kolia in Abram Room's *Bed and Sofa* [Tret′ia Meshchanskaia, 1927] and Sergeev, the head of the labour commune, in Nikolai Ekk's *Ticket to Life* [Putevka v zhizn′, 1931], one of the first Soviet sound films. On this and the casting of Babochkin, see ibid., pp. 125-7.

12 Ibid., p. 40. There is an informative description of the work of the 1920s editor of foreign films ibid., pp. 40-1.

13 Ibid., pp. 46, 56.

14 For the plot of the film see *Sovetskie khudozhestvennye fil′my. Annotirovannyi katalog*, Volume 1, *Nemye fil′my* (1918–1935), Moscow, 1961, p. 401. Some fascinating brief sequences from the film are included in the 2002 documentary on *Chapaev* in the television series *Zvezdnye gody Lenfil′ma*.

15 See the entry on the film in Ibid., p. 461. *A Personal Matter* has not survived, but Pisarevskii was able to recreate some of its imagery from materials he found in the possession of Varvara Miasnikova in 1974. See p. 81 and the pictures between pp. 64 and 65 of Pisarevskii, *Brat′ia Vasil′evy*.

16 Dolinskii, *Chapaev*, p. 23.

17 The cinematographer on *Razgrom*, Aleksandr Sigaev, would later work on *Chapaev*.

18 A. S. Deriabin (ed.), *Letopis′ rossiiskogo kino 1930–1945*, Moscow, 2007, p. 169; Dolinskii, *Chapaev. Dramaturgiia*, p. 23.

19 Ibid.

20   Pisarevskii, *Brat'ia Vasil'evy*, p. 99.
21   Among other characters developed and re-worked by the Vasil'ev
      Brothers were the vets whom Chapaev wanted to make doctors, the
      platoon commander, Zhikharev, the weaver on guard duty and the
      tall partisan who rebels. See Pisarevskii, *Brat'ia Vasil'evy*, p. 112.
      The reasons for the changes are discussed in Chapter 1 of this study.
22   For a detailed analysis of the stages of the development of the script
      see especially Pisarevskii, *Brat'ia Vasil'evy*, pp. 90-103; 'Stsenarnye
      chernoviki "Chapaeva"', *Iz istorii Lenfil'ma*, 3, 1970, pp. 230-72; and
      Dolinskii, *Chapaev*, pp. 51-66 and the tables which compare the initial
      'literary script', the version of the literary script published in the journal
      Literaturnyi sovremennik, 1933, 9, the later 'directors' script' and the film
      version, in Ibid., pp. 164-75. There have been several publications of
      the script of the film, notably in *Chapaev* in the *Shedevry sovetskogo kino*
      series, comp. L.A. Parfenov, Moscow, 1966, pp. 13-167; and in Brat'ia
      Vasil'evy, *Sobranie sochinenii*, volume 2, 1982, pp. 81-129.
23   G. and S. Vasil'evy, '"Chapaev" Furmanova i "Chapaev" na
      ekrane', *Literaturnaia gazeta*, 1935, No. 3, 15 January, p. 3; quoted
      from Brat'ia Vasil'evy, *Sobranie sochinenii*, volume 2, p. 130.
24   S. D. Vasil'ev, 'Oboronnaia kinematografiia', *Zvezda*, 1938, 2, pp.
      117-23; quoted from Brat'ia Vasil'evy, *Sobranie sochinenii*, volume 2,
      pp. 276-7.
25   The fullest version of the arguments over whether the film should
      be made with sound is in S. Vasil'ev, '"... stimula po sushchestvu net
      na fabrike"', *Iskusstvo kino*, 1991, 2, pp. 68-76 [pp. 72-4], from which
      this account is taken. It should be pointed out that this is the record
      of an interview of the Brothers on 12 January 1938 with Semen
      Dukel'skii, who had replaced Shumiatskii as the Head of the Soviet
      film industry only four days earlier, and that the interview was
      intended in part to find evidence that would discredit his
      predecessor. After the film was released the Brothers made a hybrid
      'silenced' (onemevshii) version of it to be shown at the many
      cinema installations still unequipped to show sound films.
26   Ibid.
27   *The Youth of Maxim* was released on 27 January 1935, less than
      three months after *Chapaev*. It was followed by two other films
      about Maxim.
28   For a sketch of Popov's career see V. Tsaritsyn, 'Eto sil'noe, iarkoe
      darovanie...', *Neva*, 2004, 9, pp. 250-7.
29   G. N. Vasil'ev 'Poslednie dni pered sdachei "Chapaeva"', in Brat'ia
      Vasil'evy, *Sobranie sochinenii*, volume 2, p. 460.
30   According to Pisarevskii, the Brothers agreed to the State Cinema

Directorate's demand to cut from the beginning of the scene in Colonel Borozdin's train carriage a sequence in which the Kappelite lieutenant, played by Sergei Vasil'ev, played the piano and sang the song 'Alla verdy'. Written by Count Vladimir Sollogub, this song, which was associated with the Crimean War, was popular among the White forces in the Civil War and was the anthem of one of the Tsarist Cossack Guards Regiments. On this see http://www.a-pesni.golosa.info /popular20/allaverdy.htm This sequence can be seen in the film on *Chapaev* in the *Zvezdnye gody Lenfil'ma*, series and in *Legendy mirovogo kino. Brat'ia Vasil'evy*, directed by Andrei Istratov, Telekompaniia Gamaiun, 2006. For Shumiatskii's demand that this and the scene of the 'psychic attack' be removed see Pisarevskii, *Brat'ia Vasil'evy*, pp. 163-4.

31   S. Vasil'ev, ""... stimula...", pp. 73-4. Shumiatskii's slightly different description of this evening will be discussed in Chapter 4 of this study.

Chapter 3

1   A. Ostretsov was one of the first critics to write about the importance of sound to the film's meaning, and he suggests that we pay so much attention to the troika's bells because 'in this sharp, elemental and piercing ringing we sense something of Chapaev himself and his troops': Ostretsov, 'Muzyka fil'ma', in *Chapaev. O fil'me*, Moscow, 1936, pp. 147-64 (p. 148).

2   'Chto-to svoe, rodnoe'. Vasil'ev further suggests that 'every such subliminal reaction to familiar things is advantageous' to the film-maker. See S.D. Vasil'ev, 'Stenogramma besedy vo VGIKe' [23 April 1937] in Brat'ia Vasil'evy, *Sobranie sochinenii*, volume 2, pp. 472-96 (pp. 495, 494).

3   This point was noted by the celebrated cameraman Anatolii Golovnia. See 'Fil'm "Chapaev"', in his *O kinooperatorskom masterstve*, Moscow, 1970, pp. 83-8 (p. 86).

4   This carriage is usually referred to in discussion of the film as a *tachanka*, a kind of cart encountered widely in the Ukraine and the Caucasus, and used during the Civil War both for transporting machine guns and for supporting them during use in battle, though Dmitrii Pisarevskii insists that it is just an ordinary horse-drawn carriage captured as a trophy. See his *Brat'ia Vasil'evy*, p. 154. The dominant use of the word *tachanka* leads Petr, the hero of a recent mediation upon the Chapaev cult, Viktor Pelevin's novel *The Clay Machine-Gun* [*Chapaev i Pustota*] to speculate upon its derivation and to come up with an amusing pun: 'tachanka' – 'touch Anka': Pelevin, *Chapaev i Pustota*, Moscow, 1998, p. 240.

5   This character is usually referred to in Russian-language discussions of the film as 'verzila', 'the lanky man' and I shall use this term to describe him in this study.

6   This information on the Czech corps and its role in the anti-Bolshevik fighting is taken from E. Mawdsley, *The Russian Civil War* [1987], Edinburgh, 2000, pp. 46-9, 56-7, 235. Historically the encounter between Chapaev and the Czech troops took place on the River Irgiz on 1 September 1918.

7   In this article, '"Ty" i "Vy" v Krasnoi Armii', which was published in *Izvestiia* on 19 July 1922, Trotsky further insisted that 'In the Red Army, a commanding officer may not use the familiar form to address a subordinate if the subordinate is expected to respond in the polite form. Otherwise an expression of inequality between persons would result, not an expression of subordination in the line of duty.' Quoted from William G. Rosenberg (ed.), *Bolshevik Visions: First Phase of the Cultural Revolution in Soviet Russia*, Ann Arbor, Michigan, 1984, pp. 189-90 (p. 189). Furmanov discusses the policy of levelling (uravnenie), which motivated these instructions, in chapter 12 of the novel, in which Chapaev and Klychkov 'had a relatively serious discussion about how to force the entire division to talk to each other using the familiar form of address ('razgovarivat' na "ty"') (Furmanov, *Sobranie sochinenii*, 1, p. 254).

8   Dondurei even suggests that key sequences in the film are briefly 'frozen', in order to provide the kind of iconic shot which could be transferred to a postcard or, in later years, to computer wallpaper. See 'Geroi vremeni. Chapaev', Radio Svoboda at http://www.svoboda.org/programs/cicles/hero/15.asp

9   J. Hicks, 'Educating Chapaev: from document to myth', in Stephen Hutchings and Anat Vernitski (eds), Russ*ian and Soviet Film Adaptations of Literature, 1900–2001, Screening the Word*, London and New York, 2005, pp. 44-58 (p. 51).

10   In the view of Vladimir Il'ich Lenin, 'Without Military Commissars, we would have no Red Army'. Quoted from N. A. Lebedev, 'Ocherk chetvertyi. "Chapaev"' in Iu. S. Kalashnikov, *et al.* (eds), *Ocherki istorii sovetskogo kino v trekh tomakh. Tom pervyi. 1917–1934*, Moscow, 1956, pp. 368-413 (p. 374).

11   Anna the weaver is often referred to in discussion of the film by the affectionate diminutive of her name, Anka. I have chosen to use the name in the form in which it appears in the film's opening credits. Though she bears the name of Furmanov's wife, Anna Nikitichna Steshenko, she is not involved in cultural work in Chapaev's brigade, unlike Zoia Pavlovna, the character based on

Anna Nikitichna in Furmanov's novel. Basing himself on the literary script, Iosif Dolinskii describes Anna as a woman from a worker family whose husband has been killed by White Cossacks, and suggests that the character also draws upon the figures of Marusia Riabinina and Elena Kunitsina: Dolinskii, *Chapaev*, pp. 112-14. Another suggested prototype for Anna is Mariia Andreevna Popova, about whom a documentary film, *The True Story of Anka-The Machine-Gunner*, was made in 2007. See Chapter 4 of this study.

12   O. Bulgakova, 'Stikhiia i soznatel'nost'': komandir i komissar', in her *Fabrika zhestov*, Moscow, 2005, pp. 248-52 (p. 249).

13   On the phrases from the film which have entered the language, see, for example, the lists in V.S. Elistratov, *Slovar' krylatykh slov (russkii kinematograf)*, Moscow, 1999, p. 160; and A.Iu. Kozhevnikov, *Bol'shoi slovar': Krylatye frazy otechestvennogo kino*, St Petersburg, and Moscow, 2001, pp. 376-7.

14   For Klychkov's comparison of Chapaev in the novel to the 'popular heroes' Pugachev, Razin and Ermak, see Chapter 1 of this study.

15   On the unlikelihood of this prop being given to Furmanov by chance, see, for example, V. A. Troianovskii, 'Vytesnenie istorii', *Kinovedcheskie zapiski*, 8, 1990, pp. 27-37 (p. 30).

16   Initially this scene was to be shot in the open air. But as Boris Babochkin recalls, while they were sitting in a peasant hut during the disastrously rainy location shoot of 1933, their peasant hostess brought them potatoes, which rolled out over the table, a large and ugly one at their front. One of the crew recalled the words of this scene 'The detachment marches forward, its commander in the front on his dashing steed.' When the woman brought them cucumbers another man added 'The enemy appears.' Back in Leningrad the script of this scene was changed to incorporate the emendations. See 'Chapaev', in *Istoriia sovetskogo kinoiskusstva zvukovogo perioda. Po vyskazyvaniiam masterov kino i otzyvam kritikov. Chast' 1 (1930–1941)*, Moscow, 1946, pp. 76-89 (p. 86).

17   The encounter between Petka and Anna in the film is an expression of the so called 'smychka', the connection between the town and the country, the workers and the peasants that was central to Bolshevik propaganda during these years. It is given its most famous artistic expression in Vera Mukhina's statue of the 'Worker and the Kolkhoz Woman', which was exhibited at the International Exhibition in Paris in 1937. Interestingly, though, whereas for Mukhina the town and the workers are represented by the male figure, in *Chapaev* the roles are reversed.

18   Kipling's 'Pharaoh and the Sargeant' (1897) speaks of a fighting man 'That will Maxim his oppressor as a Christian ought to do.' Belloc's

'The Fellow-Traveller', written the following year, has a colonial figure named Blood reassured that 'Whatever happens, we have got, /The Maxim gun, and they have not'.

19   On the development and use of the Maxim gun see J. Ellis, *The Social History of the Machine Gun,* London, 1993, and I. McCallum, *Blood Brothers. Hiram and Hudson Maxim : Pioneers of Modern Warfare,* London, 1999. The Maxim gun figures also figures prominently in another Civil War film, Alexander Dovzhenko's *Arsenal,* 1928.

20   Bulgakova points to the connection between the undisciplined peasant physicality of Petka and the gestural expansiveness of Chapaev: 'Stikhiia i soznatel'nost'', pp. 250-2, 263.

21   There is a wonderful parodic examination of 1930s hero cults through the figure of the cowman Vania in Alexander Medvedkin's 1936 film *The Miracle Worker* [Chudesnitsa].

22   In an informative article on the representation of the White forces in the film, E.V. Volkov suggests that Colonel Borozdin is based on the real-life figure of Major General N. N. Borodin, who led a detachment of Urals Cossacks and made the raid on Lbishchensk in September 1919 which resulted in Chapaev's death: 'Obraz kappelevtsev v fil'me Brat'ev Vasil'evykh "Chapaev"', in S. S. Balmasov *et al.* (eds), *Kappel' i kappelevtsy,* Moscow, 2003, pp. 529-44 (pp. 533-4).

23   Quoted from S. Tsimbal, *Tvorcheskaia sud'ba Pevtsova,* Leningrad and Moscow, 1957, p. 257. Pevtsov died on 25 October 1934, before the film's premiere. See the obituary in *Kino,* 28 October 1934, p. 4

24   V. I. Lenin, 'Uderzhat li bol'sheviki gosudarstvennuiu vlast''?', *Polnoe sobranie sochinenii,* fifth edition, 1958–1965, volume 34, Moscow, 1962, pp. 287-339 (p. 315).

25   Lenin, *Polnoe sobranie sochinenii,* volume 51, Moscow, 1965, p. 48. In this publication the word 'shit' (*govno*) is rendered 'g...'.

26   'Aleksandr Makedonskii tozhe byl velikii pokovodets. A zachem zhe taburetki lomat'?' In Act 1, Scene 1 of Gogol''s play the line, spoken by the mayor about the town's frenzied history teacher, reads 'Ono konechno, Aleksandr Makedonskii geroi, no zachem zhe stul'ia lomat'? ot etogo ubytok kazne': N.V. Gogol', *Polnoe sobranie sochinenii,* Moscow, 1937–1952, volume 4, 1951, p. 15. For the role of Alexander the Great in Russian literature and folklore, see E.A. Kostiukhin, *Aleksandr Makedonskii v literaturnoi i fol'klornoi traditsii,* Moscow, 1972, pp. 42-56.

27   These words are taken from a song known either as 'Ty, moriak, krasivyi sam soboiu' or as 'Po moriam, po volnam' ('By the seas, by the waves.'). It was written by Vasilii Mezhevich to be sung by a sailor in his 1839 play *Artur, ili Shestnadtsat' let spustia.* It was sung widely

during the First World War and the Civil War. In Furmanov's novel Klychkov writes that 'without a song Chapaev was always morose' and describes this song as one of his favourites, adding that he liked it most for the lines in the chorus 'By the seas, by the waves, / Here today, there tomorrow!', which 'well fitted his own partisan, wandering, restless life.' Furmanov, *Sobranie sochinenii*, 1, p. 93.

28   On the fundamental importance of the mentor – disciple relationship in the literature of the Stalinist period, and on the link of the mentor to the party, see K. Clark, *The Soviet Novel. History as Ritual*, Chicago, 1981, pp. 144-5, 168-76.

29   Henceforth in the film the degree of smartness of Chapaev's dress will be one of the ways of measuring the extent to which he has learnt the lessons in consciousness given to him by Furmanov. Marshal Dmitrii Iazov, who was the last Minister of Defence in the Soviet Union, recalls a meeting with Chapaev's widow soon after the end of the Second World War. She pronounced herself content overall with Babochkin's portrayal, but considered that in a number of ways the image of her husband had been made too primitive. In particular she insisted that Chapaev was the kind of ex-sergeant major who would never have permitted himself to be seen out of uniform. 'I do understand that it was necessary to make a feature film and make it a little more interesting in places...' Quoted from 'Russkaia kinodvadtsatka Radio Svoboda. "Chapaev"', at http://archive.svoboda.org/programs/cicles/cinema/Chapajev.asp

30   GD. Gachev, 'Natsional´nye obrazy mira – v kino', *Kinovedcheskie zapiski*, 28, 1995, pp. 69-101 (pp. 89, 95).

31   In the words of V.A. Mil´don, '*A merry-go-round* is cyclical motion, repetition, excluding any sort of history': 'Metafizika golovnogo mozga. O nekotorykh osnovnykh metaforakh sovetskogo kino 30-40-kh godov (nabliudeniia filologa)' *Kinovedcheskie zapiski*, 33, 1997, pp. 160-72 (p. 161).

32   For the thefts and the peasant women's complaint that the Red soldiers were robbing them and the suggestion that the Reds were just like the Whites, see Furmanov, *Sobranie sochineni*, 1, pp. 111-12, 184. For Babel´s admiration of the novel, see Chapter 1 of this study. For Gedali's complaint about 'revolution' and 'counter-revolution', see Babel´, *Detstvo i drugie rasskazy*, p. 126.

33   For Gachev, the arrest of Zhikharev is a prophecy of the Party's taming of the anarchic Russian spirit: 'Natsional´nye obrazy', p. 96.

34   Babochkin recalls how difficult it was to persuade the Brothers not to have Chapaev shouting throughout this scene: *Istoriia sovetskogo kinoiskusstva zvukovogo perioda*, pp. 86-7.

35   A. Dubrovin, 'Fenomen "Chapaeva" i problema khudozhestvennogo prognozirovaniia', in N. Dymshits and A. Troshin (eds), *Iz proshlogo v budushchee: proverka na dorogakh. Ob istorizme kino*, Moscow, 1990, pp. 166-82 (p. 175).

36   In a brilliant study of Chapaev's duality, Sergei Dobrotvorskii suggests that he is median figure between the troops and Furmanov, between the elements of the common people and revolutionary order, between anarchic outlaws and iron discipline, and that he therefore exhibits both the 'feminine' features of the people and the 'masculine' features of the Party; 'Thus Chapaev, resolving the film's fundamental opposition through progressive mediation, appears in the image of a mythical androgyne, a two-sexed creature': 'Fil'm "Chapaev": opyt strukturirovaniia total'nogo realizma', *Iskusstvo kino*, 1992, 11, pp. 22-8 (especially pp. 25-6).

37   According to Gachev, the right choice, in the peasant mind, would be 'Bolshevik', with its shared root with the Russian words for more, bigger, rather than 'Communist' with its incomprehensible foreign root: 'Natsional'nye obrazy', p. 99.

38   V. I. Lenin, 'Tsennye priznaniia Pitirima Sorokina' (*Pravda*, 21 November 1918), quoted from his *Polnoe sobranie sochinenii*, volume 37, 1963, pp. 188-97 (p. 195).

39   There are interesting lists of the words from the new political lexicon which peasants understood in the 1920s and those with which they had difficulty in A. Rozhkov, 'Mir krasnoarmeitsa: prevrashchenie v muzhchinu', in his *V krugu sverstnikov. Zhiznennyi mir molodogo cheloveka v sovetskoi Rossii 1920-kh godov*, Krasnodar, 2002, volume 2, pp. 59-60.

40   Furmanov's question is something of a friendly trap, since the Second, Socialist International had been dissolved in 1916. It had had its founding conference as the 'Second International' in Chur in Switzerland in October 1881, turning officially into the Socialist International at an International Socialist Congress in Paris in July 1889. The Third, Communist International (the Comintern) was founded by Lenin at a congress in Moscow in March 1919, months before the events depicted in this scene in the film.

41   Sergei Vasil'ev speaks of consciously linking Chapaev to Russian popular heroes such as Il'ia Muromets, Dobrynia Nikitych and Ermak by giving him characteristics that are 'typically Russian' and 'national' such as 'kindheartedness, infantilism, cunning and Russian resourcefulness. These are all characteristics shared with the heroes of our Russian bylina tales': 'Stenogramma besedy vo VGIKe', p. 480.

42   Marc Ferro describes this endeavour as Petka's 'ritual test', his 'rite of passage': 'The fiction film and historical analysis', in Paul Smith (ed.), *The Historian and Film*, Cambridge, 1976, pp. 80-94 (p. 92).

43   Golovnia had high praise for this scene. 'The lyrical landscapes in the scene of Petka's departure in search of a prisoner have been thought out very interestingly from the technical point of view. They were shot in the evening, into the sunlight, with artificial lighting, and in some shots the faces of the characters cover the sun. The tender tonality and soft transitions of light and shade, the generally picturesque construction of the shots gave an impression of simple, lyrical warmth; the photography of these shots harmonised with the musical accompaniment': 'Fil′m "Chapaev"', pp. 85-6. For similarly expressed praise of the music of the sequence, see Ostretsov, 'Muzyka fil′ma', p. 152.

44   The trope of the lesson taught by the Commissar then being passed on to others occurs in a number of later films, including Isidor Annenskii's *The Fifth Ocean* [Piatyi okean, 1940] and Aleksandr Stolper's *The Tale of a Real Man* [Povest′ o nastoiashchem cheloveke, 1948].

45   According to Sergei Snezhkin, the presenter of the film *Chapaev* in the *Zvezdnye gody Lenfil′ma* series, the power of this scene was such that the *Moonlight Sonata* became identified as the music of the Whites and for years it was withdrawn from the concert repertoire and not used in films.

46   M. Gor′kii, 'V. I. Lenin', (1924) in his *Polnoe sobranie sochinenii. Khudozhestvennye proizvedeniia v dvadtsati piati tomakh*, ed. L.M. Leonov *et al.*, Moscow, 1968–1976, volume 20, 'Rasskazy. Ocherki. Vospominaniia. 1924–1935', 1974, pp. 7-49 (p. 42).

47   The motif of the necessity of nocturnal watchfulness will come to play a fundamental role in the resolution of the film's plot. Like other aspects of the ethics of *Chapaev* it has its roots in the Bible, in the parable of the wise and foolish virgins who did not know when the bridegroom would come, Matthew 25:1-13.

48   On the pervasiveness of the metaphor of Soviet society as a 'great family' in Stalinist culture, see Clark, *The Soviet Novel*, pp. 114-35.

49   This information is taken from V. E. Gusev (ed.), *Pesni i romansy russkikh poetov*, Moscow and Leningrad, 1965, p. 1071. The text of the poem 'Pod zelenoiu rakitoi' is on pp. 930-31. For information on Nikolai Verevkin, see P. A. Nikolaev *et al.* (eds), *Russkie pisateli 1890–1917, biograficheskii slovar′*, Volume 1, 'A-G', Moscow, 1989, p. 423. The version of the song sung during World War Two ends: 'And tell them, raven-bird, / That I fell for my native land, / For the

Soviet border, / Under a Soviet star.' For evidence of it being sung this way in partisan brigades see N. Bialosinskaia, 'O chem shumeli brianskie lesa', in *Russkii fol'klor Velikoi otechestvennoi voiny*, Moscow and Leningrad, 1964, p. 365. In the 1930s in the Soviet Union the slang terms 'voron' and 'chernyi voron' were used to refer to the closed lorries for transporting prisoners. See V. M. Mokienko, T. G. Nikitina, *Tolkovyi slovar' iazyka Sovdepii*, second, corrected and expanded edition, Moscow, 2005, pp. 72-3. The critic Oleg Kovalov stresses the potency of this association for the film's audiences. 'In the context of the 1930s it is clear what the very theme of the "black raven" signified. Even now, when you listen to it, you shiver involuntarily. We understand that if Chapaev had not drowned in the Ural River, he would not have escaped the "black raven"'. See http://www.svoboda.org/programs /cicles /hero/15.asp

50   This is the only reference in the film to the use of planes in the Civil War. In the novel Chapaev makes constant phone calls to his commanders and has a number of fliers attached to his division. (Furmanov, *Sobranie sochinenii*, 1, p. 268). The decision to remove these 'technological' aspects of the fighting from the film is consistent with the desire to depict Chapaev and his men as the heirs of the heroes of ancient Russian history and myth.

51   The frequency with which both Chapaev and Petka, when asked if they can do something, answer simply 'Mogu', 'I can', is both a measure of their peasant self-confidence, and one of the other ways in which they are likened to the all-powerful heroes of Russian lore.

52   Gachev describes Chapaev in this scene as a 'statue, a monument to himself': 'Natsional'nye obrazy', p. 95. For Sergei Dobrotvorskii, the cloak is borrowed from Caucasian folklore, 'an allusion which it was obviously politically advantageous to make in the middle of the 1930s': 'Fil'm "Chapaev"', p. 23.

53   According to Elena Kartseva the Westerns made in the 1910s under the artistic supervision of Thomas Ince were especially successful among Soviet audiences during the 1920s. See Kartseva, 'Amerikanskie nemye fil'my v sovetskom prokate', *Kino i vremia*, 1, 1960, pp. 193-211 (pp. 196-7). Both the clear moral dichotomies and the representation of landscape in the classic Westerns were consistent with the Vasil'ev Brothers' approach in *Chapaev*. Maiia Turovskaia suggests that, during the years when Westerns were absent from Soviet screens, Chapaev was watched from generation to generation as an "Eastern": 'And of course, it was enormously popular, its popularity connected not with what was written in the papers, but with its genre features': 'Ideologicheskie klishe i

esteticheskie paralleli: kino Rossii i Ameriki, 30-40-e gody', in A. Troshin (ed.), *Close-Up. Istoriko-teoreticheskii seminar vo VGIKe*, Moscow, 1999, pp. 219-29 (p. 221).

54   S. Vasil´ev, 'Beseda v Gosudarstvennom institute kinematografii', (28 December 1934) in Brat´ia Vasil´evy, *Sobranie sochinenii v 3 tomakh*, volume 2, pp. 143-63 (pp. 158-59). Oleg Kovalov quotes Babochkin as saying that he had wanted to make Chapaev 'both naive and cruel like a wild beast'. In this context Kovalov regrets the toning down of this scene, since 'these opposites, a childlike purity and naivete and the instinctive cruelty of a wild beast are the two poles of the Russian national character, however much we might try to deny it'. http://archive.svoboda.org/programs/ cicles/cinema/Chapajev.asp

55   *Chapaev* provided a rich store of character types and plot motifs for the representation of a life and death struggle in films set in World War Two. *No Greater Love* offers a particularly striking example. As in Chapaev there is a powerful leader figure, here constructed as 'mother' rather than 'father' of her 'big family'. There are scenes set in the beautiful countryside which show audiences the Russia that is being fought over. There is a young couple in love, but they are willing to sacrifice their future happiness and one of them is killed in battle. German tanks are represented as the same kind of 'inhuman' weaponry as the Whites' armoured car at the end of *Chapaev*.

56   See the letter of Askol´dov to V. E. Baskakov, the Deputy Chairman of the State Cinema Committee, published by V. I. Fomin in 'Komissar', in his *"Polka". Dokumenty. Svidetel´stva. Kommentarii*, Moscow, 1992, pp. 46-76 (pp. 50-51).

57   Bulgakova contrasts the gestural restraint of this speech both with Chapaev's earlier speech after the return of the plundered goods and with the speech of the lanky partisan. She finds Chapaev's new manner to be evidence of his achieving the 'discipline' which Furmanov and the Party require of him: 'Stikhiia i soznatel´nost´', p. 250.

58   The theme of self-sacrifice, of 'laying down your life for your friends', another motif taken from the Bible (John 15:13), will come to dominate the later sequences of the film. On the canonical role of sacrifice in Soviet art see Esaulov, I. 'Zhertva i zhertvennost´', in Hans Günther and Evgenii Dobrenko (eds), *Sotsrealisticheskii kanon*, St Petersburg, 2000, pp. 797-802; and Clark, *The Soviet Novel*, especially pp. 72-4, 179-82

59   In the December 1934 discussion at the State Film Institute, Sergei Vasil´ev was asked why the character of Potapov came to such an abrupt end. He described the curtailing of the Potapov line in the

plot as not the will of the directors but their misfortune. He asserted that a man like Potapov would not come over to the Reds in order to work in the kitchen, and explained that the initial plan had been for him to participate in, and perish in the resistance to the 'psychic' attack: 'Beseda v Gosudarstvennom institute kinematografii', p. 159.

60   This information is taken from Mawdsley, *The Russian Civil War*, especially pp. 56-9, 65-9; I. O. Surmina, 'Vladimir Oskarovich Kappel'', in her *Samye znamenitye*, pp. 321-6; 'Kappel' Vladimir Oskarovich', in *Voennaia entsiklopediia v vos'mi tomakh*, volume 3, 'D - Kvartir'er', Moscow, 1995, p. 479; and http://news.yand ex.ru/yandsearch?cl4url=www.newsru.co.il/world/13jan2007/kapp el.html&country=Russia

61   This point was first made by B. Krusman in 'Ot dramaturgii stsenariia k dramaturgii fil'ma', in *Chapaev. O fil'me*, pp. 91-122 (p. 97).

62   Volkov, 'Obraz kappelevtsev', pp. 530-3, 539-40.

63   The writer Boris Vasil'ev (not related to the Brothers) notes the absence from the fighting at this stage of Chapaev, Furmanov and Elan: 'Vpered k "Chapaevu"!', *Ekran 1979–1980*, Moscow, 1982, pp. 22-25 (p. 24).

64   S. Vasil'ev, 'Beseda v Gosudarstvennom institute kinematografii', p. 162. Vasil'ev returns to the importance of sound in the organisation of this sequence, and specifically to the sequencing of the beating of the drum, machine-gun fire and the shouts of the Cossacks in S.D. Vasil'ev, 'Stenogramma besedy vo VGIKe', p. 494.

65   G. Vasil'ev and S. Vasil'ev, 'Stenogramma besedy v redaktsii "Komsomol'skoi pravdy"', in Brat'ia Vasil'evy, *Sobranie sochinenii*, volume 2, pp. 460-72 (p. 468).

66   For Mandel'shtam's reaction to the film, see Chapter 4 of this study.

67   Zorkaia also draws interesting parallels and contrasts with the 'Forest Army' chapter of *Doctor Zhivago* in her *Istoriia sovetskogo kino*, St Petersburg, 2005, pp. 217-20.

68   The figures are taken from Pisarevskii, *Brat'ia Vasil'evy*, p. 150. Zorkaia gives figures of two hundred cuts in Eizenshtein against Chapaev's fifty: *Istoriia sovetskogo kino*, p. 215. On the Eizenshtein connection see also Dolinskii, *Chapaev*, pp. 134-5; and M. Zak, 'Sbrosim "Chapaeva" s korablia sovremennosti...', in his *Kinoprotsess*, Moscow, 1990, pp. 24-33 (p. 32).

69   S. Vasil'ev, 'Beseda v Gosudarstvennom institute kinematografii', pp. 162-3.

70   Troianovskii, 'Vytesnenie', p. 32.

71   Vasil'ev, 'Vpered k "Chapaevu"!' p. 25.

72   Ferro, 'The fiction film', p. 92.

73   The origins of this song are obscure. It has been repeatedly re-
      worked. In 1979 it was made into a romance, sung by Al'bert
      Asadulin to music by Valerii Gavrilin.
74   Balázs's words are quoted from E. Dobrenko, 'Creation myth and
      myth creation in Stalinist cinema', *Studies in Russian & Soviet
      Cinema*, 1, 2007, 3, pp. 239-64 (p. 250).
75   Tarabukin made this point in a lecture he gave at the State Film
      Institute on 3 December 1935 about the meaning of the direction
      of movement in the film: N.M. Tarabukin, 'Smysl diagonal'nykh
      postroenii v kompozitsii fil'ma "Chapaev"', publ. N.G. Chertova,
      introduction and notes by V.V. Zabrodin, *Kinovedcheskie zapiski*, 56,
      2002, pp. 115-28 (p. 124).
76   For Valerii Fomin it is precisely because Furmanov, unlike Chapaev,
      is not given any of the heroic and humanizing qualities of the
      figures of legend and folklore that he 'does not even come close to
      the legendary Divisional Commander'. See the section 'Epos
      revoliutsii: bylinizatsiia komissarov', in his *Pravda skazki. Kino i
      traditsii fol'klora*, Moscow, 2001, pp. 96-102 (p. 102).
77   The battle around Gur'ev is also described in Boris Lavrenev's Civil
      War story 'Sorok pervyi' ('The Forty First'), in which the heroine,
      Mariutka, is a sniper in the Reds' Gur'ev Brigade, commanded by
      Commissar Evsiukov. The story was filmed by Iakov Protazanov in
      1926 and by Grigorii Chukhrai in 1956. The town of Gur'ev was
      re-named Chapaev for a period after these events.
78   Sterner critics objected to the foregrounding of the theme of the
      love affair between Petka and Anna in a film set during the Civil
      War. Mikhail Shneider called it a 'hack quotation of Americanism'
      ('remeslenicheskaia   tsitata   iz   amerikanshchiny',   in   his
      'Izobrazitel'nyi stil' brat'ev Vasil'evykh', *Iskusstvo kino*, 1938, 3, p.
      28; quoted from O. Bulgakova, 'Sovetskoe kino v poiskakh
      "obshchei modeli"', in *Sotsrealisticheskii kanon*, p. 153.
79   The poem was first published in *Russkii invalid*, 1822, No. 14, and
      reprinted in Ryleev's 1825 collection *Dumy*. For the text see, for
      example, 'Smert' Ermaka' in V. Orlov (ed.), *Dekabristy. Antologiia v
      dvukh tomakh*, volume 1, *Poeziia*, Leningrad, 1975, pp. 239-41. In
      the novel, Furmanov writes that though Chapaev and his men 'sang
      various songs, their favourites were about Stenka Razin and Ermak
      Timofeevich': Furmanov, *Sobranie sochinenii*, 1, p. 247.
80   The information here about Ermak and Kuchum is taken from I. V.
      Naumov, *The History of Siberia*, London and New York, 2006, pp. 55-
      64; and I. O. Surmina, 'Ermak Timofeevich', in her *Samye
      znamenitye*, pp. 104-13. Vasilii Surikov evoked Ermak's conquest in

his 1895 painting 'Pokorenie Sibiri Ermakom' (Ermak's Subjugation of Siberia), and 'Ermak, the Tamer of Siberia' is also depicted in popular prints (*lubki*). In Ivan Pyr'ev's 1947 film *The Tale of the Siberian Land* [Skazanie o zemle sibirskoi] the hero, Andrei Balashov, composes a 'symphonic oratorio', also called *The Tale of the Siberian Land*, which includes the story of Ermak and incorporates the words and music of 'The Death of Ermak' as sung in *Chapaev*.

81   S.D. Vasil'ev, 'Stenogramma besedy vo VGIKe', p. 495.
82   Ibid.
83   Furmanov, *Sobranie sochinenii*, 1, p. 318.
84   Furmanov, *Sobranie sochinenii*, 4, p. 208.
85   E. Chapaeva, *Moi neizvestnyi Chapaev*, p. 437.
86   Dolinskii, *Chapaev*, p. 131; Mil'don, 'Metafizika golovnogo mozga', p. 163.
87   Dubrovin, 'Fenomen "Chapaeva"', p. 171.
88   http://archive.svoboda.org/programs/cicles/cinema/Chapa jev.asp
89   V. Shklovskii, *Eizenshtein*, Moscow, 1973, p. 213.
90   For Marc Ferro 'it is Anna the worker, representing also the party, who was nothing at the beginning of the film, who henceforward gives the orders. The countryside has nothing more to do but obey the orders of the party, which represents the central authority': 'The fiction film', p. 94.
91   Convinced that the time has come 'to expose the myth' of Chapaev 'once and for all', S. S. Balmasov has recently published an archivally based account of the White raid on Lbishchensk. See Balmasov, 'Lbishchenskii reid i unichtozhenie shtaba Chapaeva, 5 sentiabria 1919 g.' *Belaia gvardiia. Al'manakh*, 5, *Beloe dvizhenie na vostoke Rossii*, Moscow, 2001, pp. 74-9 (p. 74). The article contests most of the details of the Soviet version, suggesting, for example, that Chapaev was in charge of a very large force of men and lost at least 1,500 dead and 800 captured during the raid. The White Colonel, Mikhail Il'ich Izergin, who took part in the Urals campaign of 1919, gives a similar version in his memoirs. He suggests both that Chapaev ignored intelligence of White raids, and thus was responsible for the catastrophe that ensued; and that he had with him in Lbishchensk about 2,000 men, large supplies of food and ammunition and four aeroplanes. He continues, with heavy irony, that there were also 'a large number of typists and stenographers. Clearly they do a lot of writing in Red Headquarters...' See Izergin 'Reid na Lbishchensk', *Grani*, 151, 1989, pp. 167-207 (p. 189).
92   Nikolai Tarabukin even suggests, in his study of the direction of

movement in the film, that Petka and Anna ride off in the same direction, though in fact both take a very winding path: Tarabukin, 'Smysl', p. 125.

93   The machine guns of the Reds are similarly pitted against the huge and ugly armoured car of the 'Free Ukraine' enemy forces in Dovzhenko's *Arsenal*. According to Balmasov the White armoured car is the film-makers' invention: 'Lbishchenskii reid', p. 79.

94   This sequence was actually shot on the northern Volga, near Kalinin (Tver). See Boris Babochkin's letter to his wife of 29 August 1934 in Babochkin, *Vospominaniia. Dnevniki. Pis'ma*, Moscow, 1996, p. 235; and Pisarevskii, *Brat'ia Vasil'evy*, p. 161.

95   On Chapaev's fear of being hit by a stray bullet and suffering a 'stupid death' see, in the novel, Furmanov, *Sobranie sochinenii*, 1, p. 179; and in Furmanov's diary entry of 30 April 1919, Furmanov, *Sobranie sochinenii*, 4, p. 194

96   Sergei Vasil'ev offers fulsome praise of the contribution of Popov's music to the emotional effect of the film in 'Beseda v Gosudarstvennom institute kinematografii', p. 161.

97   In his conversation in the State Film Institute in April 1937, Sergei Vasil'ev describes the 'major struggle' that took place among the film crew over how Chapaev's death should be filmed. The production designer, Makhlis, and several others wanted the scene to be shot with maximum drama, at night, in stormy waters, with wind and a noisy soundtrack, but the Brothers insisted that it should be shot calmly and without 'effects', confident that this would affect viewers more intensely: 'Stenogramma besedy vo VGIKe', pp. 484-5.

98   According to Furmanov's diary entry for 22 September 1919 Kutiakov (on whom the figure of Elan' is based) went through these places like 'an angel of vengeance, like a destroyer: he burnt all the settlements to ashes and probably left few of the inhabitants, the effect of whose spying on the Lbishchensk tragedy was so strikingly clear, alive': Furmanov, *Sobranie sochinenii*, 4, p. 210.

99   Potapov and the bearded peasant can be seen as doubles, in that they both respond to generous treatment by the Reds by coming over to the Red cause. This leads S. Freilikh to suggest that the blow struck by the bearded peasant completes the detonation caused by the crash of Potapov's fallen broom: Freilikh, 'Zolotoe sechenie ekrana', *Voprosy kinoiskusstva*, 8, 1964, pp. 58-72 (p. 71). E. V. Volkov points out that General Borodin, who made the raid on Lbishchensk on 5 September 1919, died a heroic death trying to rescue a wounded Cossack gunner, by contrast with the cowardly and humiliating death in the film of Colonel Borozdin, who takes

his name from him: 'Obraz kappelevtsev', pp. 533-4.

100   Dolinskii, *Chapaev*, p. 170; Pisarevskii, *Brat'ia Vasil'evy*, pp. 162-3.
101   Dolinskii, *Chapaev*, p. 107. Dolinskii refers on the same page to another scene intended to develop the relationship between Petka and Anna: when Furmanov was leaving, Anna asked him to take a letter for her son. On hearing this Petka asked whether she was married. To his delight, she told him that she was free. According to Dolinskii, this scene was also shot but later rejected.
102   Pisarevskii, *Brat'ia Vasil'evy*, p. 163 and one of the illustrations after p. 224.

Chapter 4

1   Shumiatskii's notes on Stalin's reactions to the films he saw at the Kremlin screenings were first published in A. S. Troshin (ed.), '"A driani podobno 'Garmon'' bol'she ne stavite?..." Zapisi besed B. Z. Shumiatskogo s I. V. Stalinym posle kinoprosmotrov. 1934 g.', *Kinovedcheskie zapiski*, 61, 2002, pp. 281-346, and continued in A. S. Troshin (ed.), '"Kartina sil'naia, khoroshaia, no ne 'Chapaev'..." Zapisi besed B. Z. Shumiatskogo s I. V. Stalinym posle kinoprosmotrov. 1935–1937 gg.', *Kinovedcheskie zapiski*, 62, 2003, pp. 115-88. They were then published, with different notes, in L. V. Maksimenkov (ed.), 'Zapisi besed B. Z. Shumiatskogo s I. V. Stalinym posle kinoprosmotrov. 7 maia 1934 g. - 26 ianvaria 1937 g.', in *Kremlevskii kinoteatr 1928–1953. Dokumenty*, Moscow, 2005, pp. 919-1053 (documents 332-94).
2   '"A driani"', p. 310.
3   Information about these later viewings of the film is taken from '"A driani"', '"Kartina sil'naia"' and *Kremlevskii kinoteatr*.
4   '"A driani"', p. 319. Kirov was killed on 1 December 1934, but one of his last tasks was to discuss the technical strengthening of the Lenfilm studios at a combined meeting of the Leningrad regional and city committees of the Party. During the discussion he asked whether anyone present had not yet seen *Chapaev*. Learning that there was, indeed, one such comrade, he told him 'For shame!' See Ia. Chuzhin, 'My poteriali chutkogo druga', *Kino*, 4 December 1934, p. 3.
5   The editorial duly followed the next day and will be discussed below.
6   '"Kartina sil'naia"', pp. 131-2, 153, 169.
7   '"Kartina sil'naia"', p. 153.
8   E. Ginzburg, *Krutoi marshrut*, Milan, 1967, p. 315; translated as *Into the Whirlwind*, London, 1967, p. 210.
9   These eloquent photographs are to be found on pp. 52-3 and 54-5 of D. King, *The Commissar Vanishes. The Falsification of Photographs*

and Art in Stalin's Russia, Edinburgh, 1997.

10 K. Simonov, 'Glazami cheloveka moego pokoleniia', *Znamia*, 1988, 4, p. 69.

11 E. Gromov, *Stalin. Vlast' i iskusstvo*, Moscow, 1998, pp. 193-4.

12 S. Dinamov, 'O groznykh dniakh bor'by', *Pravda*, 3 November 1934, p. 4

13 Kh. Khersonskii, '"Chapaev". Novaia kartina "Lenfil'm"', *Izvestiia*, 10 November 1934, p. 6

14 '"A driani"', p. 321.

15 Ibid.

16 Kinozritel', 'Kartinki v gazete i kartiny na ekrane. (O kinoretsenzii Khris. Khersonskogo v "Izvestiiakh")', *Pravda*, 12 November 1934, p. 3. The review's praise of the film as a present for the Soviet viewer directly echoes Stalin's own words.

17 'Zamechatel'noe zavoevanie' and E. Ryvina, 'Chapaev. Na prosmotre fil'ma', *Izvestiia*, 15 November 1934, p. 2

18 'Samokritika na paike (Po povodu otsenki v "Izvestiiakh" kinokartiny "Chapaev"), *Pravda*, 16 November 1934, p. 3.

19 Kh. Khersonskii, 'Pis'mo v redaktsiiu', I. Ia. Krinkin 'Ot redaktsii', *Kino*, 22 March 1935, p. 4.

20 'Ob itogakh kinofestivalia i besprintsipnoi polemike', *Pravda*, 12 March 1935, p. 1.

21 The following issues of *Kino*, on 22 and 28 November, and 4 and 10 December, would continue to report in detail on the film's progress.

22 B.V. Alpers, 'Muzhestvennaia epokha vstaet s ekrana', first in *Kino*, 16 November 1934, p. 2; reprinted, as 'Chapaev', in his *Dnevnik kinokritika 1928–1937*, Moscow, 1995, pp. 127-9.

23 S. Eizenshtein, 'Nakonets!', first published in *Literaturnaia gazeta*, 18 November 1934, is translated as 'At Last!' in S. M. Eisenstein, *Selected Works*, volume 1, *Writings, 1922–34*, ed. and transl. Richard Taylor, London, Bloomington and Indianapolis IN, 1988, pp. 296-300. Stalin, who was a great fan of *the Happy Guys* (which he called 'a very jolly and very cheerful comedy' – see '"A driani"', p. 319), considered the paper to have been irresponsible in contrasting the two films, and that 'only windbags and idlers' would give space to articles like 'At last!': see *Kremlevskii kinoteatr*, p. 969.

24 'Fil'm o podvigakh, o doblesti, o slave. Anketa "Pravdy" sredi zritelei "Chapaeva"', *Pravda*, 20 November 1934, p. 3.

25 '*Chapaeva* posmotrit vsia strana', *Pravda*, 21 November 1934, No. 320, p. 1. Reprinted in *Chapaev. O fil'me*, Moscow, 1936, pp. 5-10; translated (as 'The whole country is watching *Chapayev*'), in R. Taylor and I. Christie (eds), *The Film Factory. Russian and Soviet*

Cinema in Documents 1896–1939, London, 1988, pp. 334-5.

26   *The Film Factory*, pp. 334-5 (translation slightly modified).

27   Ibid.

28   '*Chapaeva* posmotrit vsia strana', *Pravda*, 22 November 1934, p. 6.

29   L. Kassil', 'Chapaevskie dni', *Izvestiia*, 22 November 1934, p. 4.

30   'Postanovlenie prezidiuma TsK kino-fotorabotnikov SSSR po fil'me "Chapaev"', *Kino*, 22 November 1934, p. 1.

31   '"Chapaev" v Moskve', *Izvestiia*, 23 November 1934, p. 4.

32   *Leningradskaia Pravda*, 23 November 1934, quoted from Lebedev, 'Ocherk chetvertyi', pp. 368-9.

33   Editorial of *Komsomol'skaia Pravda*, 24 November 1934, quoted from *Istoriia sovetskogo kinoiskusstva zvukovogo perioda*, p. 76.

34   Ibid.; quoted from Lebedev, 'Ocherk chetvertyi', p. 368. This a typical response from a worker viewer. See the overview of worker responses in over twenty industrial newspapers in D. Levin, 'Zavodskaia pechat' o "Chapaeve"', *Kino*, 10 December 1934, p. 2.

35   A. Orlova, 'Pis'mo pulemetchitsy', *Pravda*, 26 November 1934, p. 4.

36   'Pouchitel'naia kartina', *Krasnaia zvezda*, 27 November 1934; quoted from A. Crespi and S. de Vidovich (eds), *Prima dei codici. Il cinema sovietico prima del realismo socialista 1929/1935*, Venice, 1990, p.180.

37   G. Vasil'ev, S. Vasil'ev, 'Postanovshchiki "Chapaeva" o svoei rabote', *Izvestiia*, 29 November 1934, p. 4

38   '"Chapaev" v dome sovetskogo pisatelia', *Izvestiia*, 30 November 1934, p. 3.

39   Voroshilov's decree of 27 December is quoted from *Prima dei codici*, p. 182.

40   'O nagrazhdenii rabotnikov sovetskogo kinematografa. Postanovlenie Tsentral'nogo Ispolnitel'nogo Komiteta SSSR', *Sovetskoe kino*, 1935, 1, pp. 11-12.

41   *Pravda*, 11 January 1935, p. 1. The fourth mention of the film on the front page of the paper is in a piece entitled 'Prazdnik sovetskoi kul'tury'. Though this piece does mention other films, its greatest praise is reserved for *Chapaev*, which it calls it a 'day of celebration (*prazdnik*) for Soviet culture'.

42   B. Shumiatskii, 'Iskusstvo millionov', ibid., p. 2; V. Pudovkin, 'Nasha obshchaia pobeda', ibid., p. 3.

43   Dovzhenko's remarks were first published in *Za bol'shoe kinoiskusstvo*, Moscow, 1935, pp. 58-80 and are quoted from the re-worked version in his *Sobranie sochinenii v 4-kh tomakh*, Moscow, 1966–1969, vol. 4, 1969, pp. 43-76 (pp. 67, 49).

44   Trauberg's remarks were first published as 'Na perelome' in *Za bol'shoe kinoiskusstvo*, Moscow, 1935, pp. 50-57 and are quoted from

The Film Factory, pp. 352-54. Trauberg returned to the film in 1974, suggesting that it 'gave cinema the main thing: an enraptured viewer' ('O glavnom v nashei zhizni' [1974], quoted from L. Trauberg, *Izbrannye proizvedeniia v dvukh tomakh*, Moscow, 1988, volume 1, p. 435.

45   N. Pogodin, 'Chapaev', in D. S. Pisarevskii (ed.), *Iskusstvo millionov. Sovetskoe kino 1917-1967,* Moscow, 1958, pp. 186-97 (pp. 187, 190).

46   'Soviet authors, playwrights, poets, military workers, scientists on the film "Chapaev"', in V. Arossev (ed.), *Soviet Cinema*, Moscow, 1935, pp. 162-7 (pp. 162, 164, 166).

47   Tukhachevskii's response was published in *Chapaev. Sbornik otzyvov i statei o fil'me*, Moscow, 1935, and is quoted from L.A. Parfenov (ed.), *Chapaev. "Shedevry sovetskogo kino"*, Moscow, 1966, p. 171.

48   O. Brik, 'Znamenatel'nyi uspekh', *Znamia*, 1935, 1, pp. 187-92; quoted from Osip Brik, 'Kinopublitsistika 1930–1940-kh godov', publ. A. Valiuzhenich, *Kinovedcheskie zapiski*, 78, 2006, pp. 197-234 (pp. 213-18).

49   V. Shklovskii, 'O "Chapaeve" eshche raz', *Literaturnaia gazeta*, 1935, No. 23, 24 April 1935; quoted from the expanded edition in his *Za sorok let*, Moscow, 1965, pp. 148-54 (pp. 152, 154).

50   Iu. Olesha, 'Byt' na urovne kinoiskusstva', *Sovetskoe kino*, 1935, 3, p. 16.

51   Gor'kii's views, which regrettably are not dated, were expressed on his return home from a viewing of the film, as recorded by M. Shkapa. They are quoted from 'Maksim Gor'kii beseduet o fil'makh', *Iskusstvo kino*, 1960, 12, pp. 112-13.

52   B. Shumiatskii, *Kinematografiia millionov*, Moscow, 1935, quoted from *The Film Factory*, pp. 358-63.

53   E. Gershtein, *Memuary*, St Petersburg, 1998, p. 435.

54   The translation of this stanza is taken from G. Freidin, A *Coat of Many Colors. Osip Mandelstam and his Mythologies of Self-Presentation*, Berkeley, Los Angeles and London, 1987, p. 246.

55   Ibid. For the Russian texts of the poems see O. Mandel'shtam, *Sochineniia v dvukh tomakh*, Moscow, 1990, volume 1, pp. 214-15.

56   Pudovkin, 'Nasha obshchaia pobeda', p. 3.

57   I. D. Gotseridze, 'Istoki moego opyta', in *Rasskazy stroitelei metro*, Moscow, 1935; quoted from http://www.metro.ru/library/rass kazy_stroitelei_metro/11.html

58   Pisarevskii, *Brat'ia Vasil'evy*, p. 166.

59   S. Dukel'skii, 'Sovetskaia kinematografiia v tret'em piatiletii', *Pravda*, 10 February 1939, p. 4.

60   N. Zorkaia, '"Chapaev" i teplota', in her *Krutitsia, vertitsia shar*

goluboi... *(Desiat' shedevrov sovetskogo kino)*, Moscow, 1998, pp. 79-93 (p. 81).

61   The Central Committee Resolution 'O kinonegativnom fonde' is quoted from V. Malyshev, *Gosfil'mofond: Zemlianichnaia poliana*, Moscow, 2005, pp. 60-1. The document is published in full in *Kremlevskii kinoteatr*, pp. 295-7.

62   I. Vaisfel'd is the first to list examples of this phenomenon in his 'Khudozhestvennye techeniia sovetskogo kino i "Chapaev"', in *Chapaev. O fil'me*, p. 191. These winged phrases' have also been discussed in Chapter 3 of this study.

63   Amusingly Babochkin reports the first of these stories as an anecdote and the second as 'what really happened' and was reported to him by the directors of Moscow cinemas; see *Chapaev. "Shedevry sovetskogo kino"*, p. 206. Among others to report the first anecdote is the writer and scriptwriter Valerii Frid. See his 'Kinoteatr moego detstva', *Iskusstvo kino*, 1997, 8, pp. 20-2 (p. 22).

64   'Narodnyi geroi Vasilii Ivanovich Chapaev 1919–1939', *Pravda*, 5 September 1939, p. 4.

65   In 'Shel Chapaev' (Chapaev was marching), a new song published in the newspaper *Krasnaia zvezda* on 23 October 1940, p. 4, for example, Chapaev meets Frunze and reports on his readiness and that of his men for mortal battle. For analysis of several of the new tales about Chapaev see Frank J. Miller, *Folklore for Stalin: Russian Folklore and PseudoFolklore of the Stalin Era*, Armonk, New York and London, 1990.

66   This information is taken from the 2002 documentary film *Nikolai Starostin. Otets 'Spartaka'*, directed by Evgenii Bogatyrev.

67   I. Babel', untitled piece, published as '(Furmanov)' in his S*ochineniia v 2-kh tomakh*, volume 2, pp. 359-61 (p. 360). For Babel''s involvement in earlier attempts to film the novel see Chapter 1 of this study.

68   *Chapaev. O fil'me*, Moscow, 1936. Reference has been made to the articles in this book in Chapter 3 of this study.

69   'Fashistskaia gadina unichtozhena'; translated in *The Film Factory*, pp. 387-9. Shumiatskii was executed on 29 July 1938. For a revealing survey of his career, see R. Taylor, 'Ideology as mass entertainment: Boris Shumyatsky and Soviet cinema in the 1930s', in R. Taylor and I. Christie (eds), *Inside the Film Factory. New Approaches to Russian and Soviet Cinema*, London and New York, 1991, pp. 193-216.

70   Shneider, M. 'Izobrazitel'nyi stil' brat'ev Vasil'evykh', p. 28. Shneider further drew attention to the film's 'defeats and failures', which he put down to 'elements of hack work and formal borrowings', Ibid., p. 29.

71   *Vecherniaia Moskva*, 1942, No. 33. Mokrousov later returned to this work, producing a second version in 1942, which was staged with immense success at the Moscow Music Theatre, and a third version in 1961.

72   D. Vertov, 'V zashchitu khroniki' (1939), quoted from his *Stat'i. Dnevniki. Zamysly*, ed. S. Drobashenko, Moscow, 1966, p. 153.

73   S. Eizenshtein, 'Eshche raz o stroenii veshchei', *Iskusstvo kino*, 1940, 6, pp. 27-32; a second variant of this article was published in a re-worked version in his *Izbrannye sochineniia v shesti tomakh*, Moscow, 1964–1971, vol. 3, 1964, pp. 234-50. The article is translated in S. Eisenstein, *Nonindifferent Nature*, transl. Herbert Marshall, Cambridge, 1987, pp. 200-15. The two quotations are modified from passages on pp. 209 and 211.

74   Reported in 'V prezidiume TsIK Soiuza SSR', *Pravda*, 28 February 1935, p. 1.

75   M. Erlikh, 'Ukrainskii Chapaev', *Pravda*, 5 March 1935, p. 6.

76   '"Kartina sil'naia"', p. 127. The notes of this meeting are also extremely interesting in showing the precariousness of the Vasil'ev Brothers' own position as court favourites. Zhdanov repeatedly (and apparently without justification) attacks Sergei Vasil'ev for 'giving himself airs' and 'loafing around', and Shumiatskii concedes that 'in part he does have these qualities'. Stalin replies that however successful they have been previously this will not prevent a 'correct assessment' being made of any future work. Ibid., p. 128.

77   See *Kremlevskii kinoteatr*, pp. 267-8, 1030-1 for reports on these discussions.

78   A. Dovzhenko, 'Uchitel' i drug khudozhnika', *Iskusstvo kino*, 1937, 10, pp. 15-16; translated as 'The Artist's Teacher and Friend', *The Film Factory*, pp. 383-5.

79   This letter is quoted from G. Liber, *Alexander Dovzhenko. A Life in Soviet Film*, London, 2002, p. 154. There is an excellent discussion of the arduous gestation of the film, ibid., pp. 154-62. For comparisons of *Chapaev* and *Shchors*, see, for example, Pisarevskii, *Brat'ia Vasil'evy*, pp. 188-90; Fomin, *Pravda skazki*, pp. 96-102; and Dobrenko, 'Creation myth', pp. 252-60.

80   This letter is quoted from V. Fomin, 'Belorusskie khroniki', *Kinoforum*, 2004, 3, pp. 49-59 (p. 53). The letter is also published in full in *Kremlevskii kinoteatr*, p. 317.

81   On these two films see Dobrenko, 'Creation myth', pp. 260-1.

82   'Na ekranakh Soiuza, Frantsii i SShA', *Pravda*, 20 November 1934, p. 3.

83   Information on the American and British reception of the film is

taken from J. Hicks, 'The international reception of early Soviet sound cinema: *Chapaev* in Britain and America', *Historical Journal of Film, Radio and Television*, 25, 2005, 2, pp. 273-89.

84   Richard Watts Jr in the *New York Herald Tribune* and Andre Senwald in the *New York Times*, quoted from Ibid., pp. 276-7.

85   V. Romm, '"Chapaev" v Amerike (Ot sobstvennogo korrespondenta "Izvestii"), *Izvestiia*, 20 February 1935, p. 2

86   VNV, 'Sovetskie fil'my v N'iu-Iorke', *Pravda*, 2 March 1935, p. 5.

87   This material on the British reception of the film is taken from Hicks, 'The international reception of early Soviet sound cinema', pp. 278-80.

88   Ibid., pp. 280-4.

89   G. Adamovich, 'Chapaev', *Poslednie novosti*, 6 December 1935, p. 4.

90   B. Mikhailov, '"Chapaev" na ekranakh Parizha (Po telefonu ot parizhskogo korrespondenta "Pravdy")', *Pravda*, 15 December 1935, p. 5. There is further quotation of positive French reaction in '"Chapaev" v Parizhe', *Kino*, 1936, 1, p. 3.

91   '"Chapaev" vo Frantsii', *Izvestiia*, 28 May 1936, p. 4.

92   G. Sadoul, 'Po povodu neskol'kikh frantsuzskikh fil'mov', *Iskusstvo kino*, 1937, 2; quoted from *Iskusstvo kino*, 2001, 1, p. 46.

93   On the earlier banning, see Pisarevskii, *Brat'ia Vasil'evy*, p. 195; on the later release see *Le Peuple Dimanche*, Algiers, 20 September 1964, quoted from *Chapaev. "Shedevry sovetskogo kino"*, p. 187.

94   Pisarevskii, *Brat'ia Vasil'evy*, p.195.

95   H. Thomas, *The Spanish Civil War*, Harmondsworth, 1965, pp. 798-99; p. 587, note 1; p. 438, note 4.

96   I. Erenburg, 'Vozle Teruelia', *Izvestiia*, 3 March 1937; quoted from its publication as 'Pod Teruelem' in 'Ispanskie reportazhi. 1936–1939', in his *Sobranie sochinenii v vos'mi tomakh*, Moscow, 1990–2000, volume 4, 1991, pp. 465-7 (pp. 465, 466). Erenburg wrote movingly of the feelings the screening aroused in him in the poem 'V kastil'skom nishchenskom selen'e', first published in *Znamia*, 1939, 7-8, p. 234; reprinted in Erenburg, *Stikhotvoreniia*, Leningrad, 1977, pp. 139-40.

97   M. Kol'tsov, 'Ispanskii dnevnik', in his *Izbrannye proizvedeniia v trekh tomakh*, Moscow, 1957, volume 3, pp. 37-8.

98   Ibid. p. 242. There may be an element of exaggeration in Erenburg and Kol'tsov's reports for Soviet audiences.

99   B. Knox, *Premature Anti-Fascist*. Abraham Lincoln Brigade Archives – Bill Susman Lecture Series. King Juan Carlos I of Spain Center – New York University, 1998. http://www.alba-valb.org/lectures/1998_knox_bernard.html

100 Information from an October 1944 report to Ivan Bol'shakov, the

then head of the State Film Committee, on the export of Soviet films over the last twenty years. Quoted from Valerii Fomin (ed.), *Kino na voine. Dokumenty i svidetel'stva*, Moscow, 2005, pp. 655-6. An even larger figure is quoted by Boris Shumiatskii in a 1936 note to Viacheslav Molotov in which he reports that he has received a letter stating that 'In two and a half months over two million people in Spain have seen the film...' (*Kremlevskii kinoteatr*, p. 376.

101   Pisarevskii, *Brat'ia Vasil'evy*, p. 199.

102   *Kino na voine*, p. 88.

103   Ibid., pp. 60-3.

104   Pisarevskii, *Brat'ia Vasil'evy*, p. 171.

105   R. Iurenev, '*Chapaev*', *Iskusstvo kino*, 1964, 11, pp. 10-17 (p. 11).

106   'B'emsia my zdorovo / Kolem otchaianno – / Vnuki Suvorova / Deti Chapaeva.' The words are by Samuil Marshak. Kukryniksy is the pseudonym of the group of artists Mikhail Kupriianov, Porfirii Krylov and Nikolai Sokolov. The poster can be viewed at http://www.plakaty.ru/posters?id=1117&cid=5

107   H. Fyfe, 'The Russian Soldier', *Picture Post*, Vol. 12, No. 3, 19 July 1941, pp. 9-13 (p. 9). There is no mention of Chapaev in the article or, seemingly, awareness of the source of the image.

108   Dilys Powell's review, of 31 May 1942, is quoted from Pisarevskii, *Brat'ia Vasil'evy*, p. 197. See also Hicks, 'The international reception of early Soviet sound cinema', p. 280. When the film was shown at the National Film Theatre in London in 1962, Dilys Powell wrote in the NFT booklet: 'We are in luck with the present revival. *Chapayev* is still an astonishing work, humane, touching, tremendous.'

109   See Miller, *Folklore for Stalin*, p. 90

110   *Chapaev. "Shedevry sovetskogo kino"*, pp. 206-7.

111   G. Roshal', 'Istoriko-biograficheskii fil'm', *Iskusstvo kino*, 1948, 5; quoted from Iskusstvo kino, 2001, 1, p. 48.

112   A. Bazin, 'Le mythe de Stalin dans le cinéma soviétique', *Esprit*, 17, No. 170, July-August 1950, pp. 210-35. The quotations here are modified from those in 'The Myth of Stalin in the Soviet cinema' in B. Cardullo (ed.), *Bazin at Work. Major Essays and Reviews from the Forties and Fifties*, New York and London, 1997, pp. 23-40 (p. 26). The comparison with Stalin is in Ibid., pp. 33-34.

113   Lebedev, 'Ocherk chetvertyi', p. 413.

114   Pogodin, 'Chapaev', p. 187.

115   M. Romm, '"Itak, segodnia my zaimemsia istoriei sovetskogo kino". Lektsiia M.I Romma na kursakh kinorezhisserov "Mosfil'ma", 1957 g.', publ. V.V. Zabrodin, *Kinovedcheskie zapiski*, 50, 2001, pp. 111-35 (pp. 126-27).

Notes 131

116 The interview with Tarkovskii is published in A. Lipkov, *Professiia ili prizvanie*, Moscow, 1991, pp. 9-31 (p. 25).

117 See, for example, Iurenev, '*Chapaev*' and B. Babochkin, 'Tridtsat´ let spustia', *Novyi mir*, 1964, 11, pp. 162-76.

118 F. Abramov, diary entry of 8 January 1967, first published in *Izvestiia*, 3 February 1990, No. 35, p. 3; quoted from M. Zak, 'Sbrosim "Chapaeva"', p. 30. It is of course significant that Abramov's words were not published until just before the fall of the Soviet Union.

119 A. Krasniashchikh, 'Igraem v kino. Personazhi kul´tovogo kino v detskikh igrakh i anekdotakh', *Iskusstvo kino*, 2005, 2, pp. 77-85 (p. 80).

120 Genis is quoted from http://archive.svoboda.org/programs/cicles/cinema/Chapajev.asp

121 Despite this, Boris Babochkin so disliked the anecdotes that he published an article attacking them. See K. B. Sokolov, 'Gorodskoi fol´klor protiv ofitsial´noi kartiny mira', in N. M. Zorkaia (ed.), *Khudozhestvennaia zhizn´ Rossii 1970-kh godov kak sistemnoe tseloe*, St Petersburg, 2001, pp. 225-51 (p. 247), quoting S. Rassadin, 'Anekdot – da i tol´ko', *Novaia gazeta*, 1998, 51, 28 December – 3 January 1999, p. 15. There is further evidence of Babochkin's disapproval of the phenomenon in the documentary film *Podlinnaia istoriia Anki-pulemetchitsy*, discussed below.

122 Pelevin is quoted from http://archive.svoboda.org/programs/cicles/cinema/Chapajev.asp For his own 'image of another Chapaev', see below.

123 This anecdote is among several recounted by Bruce Adams in his *Tiny Revolutions in Russia*, New York and London, 2005, pp. 117-21 (p. 118). There are several more in Seth Graham's study (see note 124), but sadly many of the best of them lose in the translation.

124 S. Graham. *A Cultural Analysis of the Russo-Soviet Anekdot*, p. 184; quoted from http://etd.library.pitt.edu/ETD/available/etd-11032003-192424/unrestricted/grahamsethb_etd2003.pdf

125 Ibid., pp. 185-86.

126 Khutsiev's words were published in *Sovetskaia kul´tura*, on the fiftieth anniversary of the film's release, 7 November 1984, and are quoted from Dubrovin, 'Fenomen "Chapaeva"', p. 166; and from L.A. Parfenov, 'Revoliutsiia, propisavshaiasia v sovremennosti', in L.M. Budiak (ed.), *Istoriia otechestvennogo kino*, Moscow, 2005, pp. 218-39 (p. 223).

127 The group often represented their name by preceding the letters paev with the iconic image of the bearded and bereted Che. For this cartoon and some of the group's other drawings and collages

of Chapaev see *Seans*, 16, 1997, pp. 12-13.

128 *Pro Chapaia. Narodnyi skaz*, designed by Dmitrii Drozdetskii, St Petersburg, 2000.

129 The links between *Wild East* and *Chapaev* are considered in L. Attwood, 'Men, machine guns and the mafia. Post-Soviet cinema as a discourse on gender', *Women's Studies International Forum*, 18, 1995, pp. 513-21 (pp. 517-18).

130 'Um i vlast', sila i mudrost'... IV (Vneocherednoi) s''ezd kinematografistov Rossii', *Iskusstvo kino*, 1998, 8, pp. 5-25 (p. 7).

131 Tolstaia's speech was published in *Dom kino*, March 1990 and is quoted from *Prima dei codici*, p. 181.

132 The *Kinopravda*? screening was broadcast on the first channel of Russian television on 23 April 1994.

133 A. Levkin, 'Chapaev. Mesto rozhdeniia: Riga (Novoe o G.I. Gurdzhieve)', *Kommentarii*, 1992, 1; reprinted in his *Tsyganskii roman*, St Petersburg, 2000, pp. 56-72.

134 V. Aksenov, 'Korabl' mira Vasilii Chapaev', *Znamia*, 1995, 1, pp. 11-20.

135 *Chapaev i Pustota* (the second name is Petka's surname in the novel, but is also the Russian word for emptiness), was first published in the journal *Znamia* 1996, Nos. 4 and 5. It appeared the same year in Moscow in book form. It has been widely discussed, notably in R. Chitnis, *Literature in Post-Communist Russia and Eastern Europe. The Russian, Czech and Slovak fiction of the Changes, 1988–1998*, London and New York, 2005, 154-9; and A. Mørch, 'Reality as myth: Pelevin's *Čapaev i Pustota*', *Scandoslavica*, 51, 2005, pp. 61-79.

136 A. Shchigolev, 'Dezha viu, ili Kuda privodiat mechty', *Iskusstvo kino*, 2001, 3, pp. 33-35. Balabanov uses the song 'Black Raven' from *Chapaev* in his 2002 film *Voina* (War).

137 On *Soviet Park* see Dobrenko, E. http://www. kinokult ura.com/2007/15r-sovietpark.shtml

138 *Neizvestnyi Furmanov*, Kupriianovskii's publication of Furmanov's diaries, and hence his confirmation of the love triangle, was discussed in Chapter 1 of this study. For an example of the distress the film caused, see T. Petrova, O. Kruglova, P. Korobtsov, '"Chistyi, blagorodnyi chelovek". Pervyi kanal oklevetal Chapaeva', *Sovetskaia Rossiia*, 27 September 2003.

139 Other interesting documentary films include *Chapaev. Legenda fil'ma*, produced by Sergei Levin, 1999; a film about *Chapaev* directed by Nataliia Urvacheva for the television series *Zvezdnye gody Lenfil'ma*, 2002; and *Brat'ia Vasil'evy*, directed by Vladimir Nepevnyi, 2002.

140 V. Mel'nikov, *Zhizn'. Kino*, St Petersburg, 2005, pp. 50-62.

Further Reading

In English:

Crofts, S. 'Ideology and form: Soviet Socialist Realism and *Chapayev'*, *Essays in Poetics*, 2, 1977, 1, pp. 43-59.

Dobrenko, E. 'Creation myth and myth creation in Stalinist cinema', *Studies in Russian & Soviet Cinema*, 1, 2007, 3, pp. 239-64.

Haynes, J. *New Soviet Man. Gender and Masculinity in Stalinist Soviet Cinema*, Manchester, 2003, pp. 154-80.

Hicks, J. 'Educating Chapaev: from document to myth', in S. Hutchings and A. Vernitski (eds), *Russian and Soviet Film Adaptations of Literature, 1900–2001, Screening the Word*, London and New York, 2005, pp. 44-58.

Hicks, J. 'The international reception of early Soviet sound cinema: *Chapaev* in Britain and America', *Historical Journal of Film, Radio and Television*, 25, 2005, 2, pp. 273-89.

Hutchings, S. '*Chapaev*. Georgii and Sergei Vasil´ev, USSR, 1934', in B. Beumers (ed.) *The Cinema of Russian and the Former Soviet Union*, London, 2007, pp. 69-77.

Shumiatskii, B. [on *Chapaev* from his book *Kinematografiia millionov*] in R. Taylor and I. Christie (eds), *The Film Factory. Russian and Soviet Cinema in Documents 1896–1939*, London, 1988, pp. 358-63.

In Russian:

Chapaev. O fil´me Moscow, 1936.

Chapaev. "Shedevry sovetskogo kino", Moscow, 1966.

Dolinskii, I. *Chapaev. Dramaturgiia*, Moscow, 1945.

Dobrotvorskii, S. 'Fil'm "Chapaev": opyt strukturirovaniia total'nogo realizma', *Iskusstvo kino*, 1992, 11, pp. 22-28.

Gachev, G.D. 'Natsional'nye obrazy mira – v kino', *Kinovedcheskie zapiski*, 28, 1995, pp. 69-101 (on *Chapaev* pp. 86-101).

Pisarevskii, D. Brat'ia Vasil'evy, Moscow, 1981.